TEACHER'S RESOU

Testing KS3
ENGLISH
Skills & Practice

YEAR 7

WRITING

READING

Ray Barker ◆ Christine Moorcroft

Published in 2003 by:
Nelson Thornes Ltd
Delta Place
27 Bath Road
CHELTENHAM
GL53 7TH
United Kingdom

03 04 05 06 07 / 10 9 8 7 6 5 4 3 2 1

A catalogue record for this book is available from the British Library

ISBN 0 7487 7137 9

Developed and produced by Start to Finish
Page make-up and illustration by Barking Dog Art
Printed and bound in Great Britain by Antony Rowe

Acknowledgements

The tests, questions and advice in this series are based upon official test materials sent to schools, but are not reproductions of these tests. The official testing process is supported by guidance and training for teachers by the Qualifications and Curriculum Authority (QCA) to use in setting, marking tests and interpreting results. The results achieved by taking the tests in this book may not be the same as are achieved in the official tests.

We gratefully acknowledge permission to include the following copyright material: **Test Paper 7:** extract on The Great Storm of 1987 published on www.met-office.gov.uk website, © Crown copyright, Met Office, reproduced under Licence Number 20020047 by permission of the Met Office; Ted Hughes: 'Wind' from *The Hawk in the Rain* (1957), reprinted by permission of the publishers, Faber & Faber Ltd; Clive King: extract from *The Night the Water Came* (Longman Young Books, 1973), reprinted by permission of David Higham Associates; **Test Paper 8:** Robert C. O'Brien: extract from *Mrs Frisby and the Rats of NIMH* (Gollancz/Hamish Hamilton, 1972), copyright © Robert C. O'Brien 1971, reprinted by permission of Penguin Books Ltd; James Kirkup: 'The Caged Bird in Springtime' from *Collected Shorter Poems* (University of Salzburg Press, 1997), reprinted by permission of the author; extract from campaign literature 'UK Zoos: Fit for Life?', reprinted by permission of the Born Free Foundation; **Test Paper 9:** Richmal Crompton: extract from *Just William on Holiday* (Macmillan, 1996), reprinted by permission of the publisher; extracts from the National Rail website, www.nationalrail.co.uk, reprinted by permission of the Association of Train Operating Companies.

Although we have tried to obtain copyright permissions before publication this has not been possible in every case. If notified, the publisher agrees to make the necessary arrangements to rectify the situation.

Contents

Introduction

Pupils need knowledge, understanding and skills to be able to deal with national tests; to develop these they need practice. That practice should provide guidance to help the pupils to develop their knowledge and skills. Many books seek to deal with the skills; they are also developed during normal English lessons. This series provides practice which develops pupils' knowledge, understanding and skills in an easy-to-use format, providing texts which are intended to be teacher-mediated (and which provide hints and tips) and others which the pupils should work on alone. The series provides step-by-step advice and support to encourage the pupils.

The Pupil Book consists of six complete test papers. Each unit consists of four sections, allowing for differentiation and building upon success. For example:

- Reading test 1: Some basics … provides more assistance, often on a shorter or an easier passage
- Reading test 2: Extending your skills … develops skills using a longer passage or more complex skills
- Reading test 3: Over to you … allows the pupils more scope to deal with the passage alone, providing simple help only
- Writing test: The real thing … deals with the two required writing assignments, providing planning and writing formats.

Each unit leads pupils through skills such as:
- describing, selecting and retrieving information from the text, using quotation and reference
- deducing, inferring and interpreting information and events from the text
- commenting on structure and organisation of texts, with reference to grammatical and presentational features
- commenting on the writer's use of language, and referring to grammatical and literary features at word and sentence level
- identifying and commenting on the writer's purposes and viewpoints, and the effect this has on the reader.

The work in the six units also provides valuable strategies for ordering and writing answers. All genres are covered, with the emphasis on cross-curricular work using non-fiction, to allow for variety in the tests. Sections will highlight basic word- and sentence-level issues when and where relevant.

The answers to the tests in the Pupil Book are provided here in the Teacher's Resource, which also provides:
- advice for pupils when taking tests
- assistance for teachers when marking tests
- three photocopiable supplementary Key Stage 3 tests (but without the detailed hints and suggestions which were given in the Pupil Book).

This series offers English Departments a way of dealing with national tests within a pedagogically sound framework. It anticipates any concerns that they are simply 'teaching for the test', because the approaches taken and the skills covered in the series are key and generic.

Year 7 tests for Key Stage 3

The Year 7 tests for Key Stage 3 now complement the *Framework for teaching English*. The Writing test links with the word-level, sentence-level and text-level structure of the *Framework for teaching English*, and the Reading test requires pupils to show their understanding of how texts work. In addition, the tests focus on continuity and progression from the Key Stages 1 to 2 strategy to the top ranges of Key Stage 3. They aim to be challenging in their questions and in their use of a variety of genres, adding a cross-curricular dimension. There are two equally weighted papers: Reading and Writing.

Reading

75 minutes
15 minutes' reading time

This paper tests a pupil's ability to:
- describe, select and retrieve information
- deduce, infer and interpret information
- comment on organisation and structure (including grammar and presentation)
- comment on a writer's use of language (including literary features at word and sentence level)
- comment on a writer's purpose and views, and their effect on the reader.

The test consists of three passages, from different genres, on one theme. The questions are marked out of 50.

Writing

75 minutes

There are two Writing tests:
- A major task (a longer, more open-ended piece). Pupils should spend a longer time on this question. It is worth 30 marks.
- A minor task (a shorter, more specific and succinct piece). Pupils should not write too much for this question. It is worth 20 marks.

The Writing tests are linked to the theme of the Reading test.
Planning formats are provided to help pupils to organise their writing.
Teachers can read the tasks through with the pupils.

Each Writing task tests a pupil's ability to:
- write imaginative, interesting texts
- write appropriately to topic, audience and purpose
- organise and structure texts appropriately
- write and construct coherent paragraphs
- write clear and varied sentences for effect
- write with technical accuracy, using appropriate grammar and punctuation
- select appropriate vocabulary
- spell words correctly.

Spelling is assessed within the Writing test, not separately.

Important test strategies

Remember

- Keep an eye on the time! When you are practising the tests, spend a little longer at first, but aim to become quicker. Remember: you will not be given any extra time in the real test. When the invigilator says 'Put your pens down' – that's it!

- Which question is worth more marks? Spend more time on that question – but not *too* much more time. Write the time you need to spend on each question alongside it on the question paper.

- Look at how many marks are allocated. Try to make that many points. If there are 3 marks, make 3 points (and back them up with evidence). It won't be that easy, but it will keep you looking for information, and writing until the end.

- Don't ignore the help you are given on the paper. The examiners tell you what to think about. Use these prompts as a plan for your own reading and writing.

- Underline the key points, or highlight them in some way – or whatever works best for you. You can write on the exam papers, and it is helpful to do so. You have 15 minutes' reading time to start with – no writing is allowed then – but you can start to get ideas and remember where key points are to be found. When you go back to underline things you will also be reading it again.

- Make your notes before you start to write. The aim is not to fill in as many sheets in your answer booklet as possible. You only get the one chance, so think about what you want to write before you put your pen to paper.

- When you write your answer, write in sentences; don't just copy your notes on to the paper. Don't be afraid to cross things out and write them again. It is important to be neat – but it is more important to say what you mean.

- Write in paragraphs – even leave a line between them; this makes your work easier to read. One rule should always be: make life easy for the examiners!

- Use quotations – but not huge chunks! You are using quotations to back up your points, not to fill up the answer booklet. It is best to quote short phrases and single words.

- If you get stuck on a question, leave it for the moment – but remember to leave a page empty in your answer booklet in case you want to go back.

- If you have time left, go back over your answers.

Good luck!

The Major Writing task: criteria for marking

Marked out of 30.
Follow the sequence of these sections to build a picture of a pupil's strengths and weaknesses.

Criteria	Marks
Sentences and punctuation	
● Ideas mostly linked. Simple conjunctions such as *and* and *but* used. Simple and compound sentences. Little variation in word order; subjects and verbs repeated. Piece lacks language variety. Basic punctuation marks: full stops, capital letters, question marks used correctly.	1
● Sentence construction is varied: for example, use of relative clauses, *who* and *which*. Complex conjunctions used for effect: for example, *if* to suggest alternative, *because* to suggest cause and effect. Commas used correctly.	2
● Variety of sentences: simple, compound, complex. Phrases and clauses used to convey interesting information. Different sentence types: questions, commands. Verbs used more creatively: *would*, *could*, *can*. Punctuation used correctly to demarcate sentences.	3
● Sentences contain complex grammatical structures, to vary length and meaning. Sentences used to create deliberate effects, and punctuation supports this: bullet points, brackets, dashes.	4
● Sentences show control and variation. Punctuation is accurate, creates deliberate effects and avoids ambiguity.	5
Paragraphs and structure	
● Some ideas are linked through the subject or topic. Use of some paragraphs, but not always accurate. Ideas tend to be listed and not grouped appropriately.	1
● Paragraphs are used. They open with a topic sentence and contain examples to develop and back up the thesis. Ideas not well developed.	2
● Some logical sequence of paragraphs to support the argument or idea. The writer introduces and concludes the text. Paragraphs of different lengths deliberately used for persuasion or development.	3
● Content is fairly detailed and well organised. Sophisticated connectives: for example, for relationships (*on the other hand*). Topic sentences used in the most effective places. Introductory paragraph directs the thought process and purpose. Conclusion rounds off ideas.	4
● Paragraphs are varied and the writer is obviously in control of his or her ideas. Structure held together by sophisticated use of connectives. Paragraphs varied in structure to create impact.	5
Purpose and effect	
● Written form appropriate and shows some awareness of the reader. Content mainly relevant.	1–3
● The form is used in a lively and correct way. The writer is aware that he or she has to interest the reader. Reasons given to support views, or details reinforce purpose.	4–6
● Detailed attention given to the subject in an appropriate style for the purpose of the writing. Reasons or details are clear and interest the reader. Style is controlled and fairly convincing; viewpoint is clear.	7–9
● Text is structured effectively and the style is appropriate to purpose. Writer uses details persuasively. Writer's viewpoint is consistent throughout.	10–12
● Tone and content of the written piece are carefully controlled and sustained. Written piece is of interest to the reader. Content is carefully and relevantly selected to support purpose of text.	13–15
Spelling	
● The spelling of simple words is on the whole accurate.	1
● The spelling of simple and common words of more than one syllable is usually correct.	2
● The spelling of words containing complex regular patterns is usually accurate.	3
● Most spelling is correct.	4
● Nearly all spelling is correct.	5

The Minor Writing task: criteria for marking

Marked out of 20.
Follow the sequence of these sections to build a picture of a pupil's strengths and weaknesses.

Criteria	Marks
Vocabulary	
● A range of nouns and adjectives is used, but no real variety. Little evidence of choosing words for meaning and effect. Not using vocabulary precisely to enhance meaning.	1
● Attempt to use vocabulary to create some effects and interest the reader. Adjectives and adverbs begin to add detail to descriptions. Choice of verbs becoming more accurate.	2
● Word choice is appropriate to the form of writing and serves to advance the purpose of the writer. Verbs, adjectives and adverbs are used to add to the effects required.	3
● A full range of vocabulary is used, from simple to the most complicated, in order to achieve the required effects and interest the reader. Writer is aware of how to manipulate language through word-play and patterning. The tone and authorial stance are assisted by the consistent use of adjectives and adverbs.	4
Sentences and paragraphs	
● Ideas and phrases linked by simple conjunctions; mainly simple or compound sentences. Writer does not vary word order or sentence construction. Basic punctuation and capital letters are used to demarcate sentences in a simple paragraph structure.	1–2
● Writer uses varied sentences (relative clauses use *who* and *which* appropriately). Verb tenses and pronouns used consistently. More sophisticated forms of punctuation: for example, commas used correctly. Paragraphs used and show that the author is selecting detail in a planned way.	3–4
● More complex and compound sentences used. Writer uses phrases and clauses to add detail and information. The meaning in sentences is more precise through the correct use of pronouns, tenses and qualifying adverbs. Paragraphs are used and material in them is sequenced effectively.	5–6
● The writer manipulates the length and focus of sentences to achieve the required effect. Writer is aware of how grammatical structures can be used to achieve these effects. Punctuation is varied and used correctly. Paragraphs are varied in length and structure to contribute effectively to the piece of writing as a whole.	7–8
Purpose and effect	
● The form of writing shows some awareness of the reader. Writer uses some stylistic features to achieve an effect. Content chosen is mostly relevant.	1–2
● Text has a sense of purpose relevant to the form used and aims to interest the reader. Writer is aware of stylistic devices such as patterning and repetition to achieve particular effects. The topic is covered with relevant detail, but writing tends not to be original.	3–4
● Writer shows a secure grasp of the form of writing, establishing purpose and sense of context for reader. Concepts such as setting and character are developed. Stylistic devices are used to communicate meaning. Narration and description are used together but writer reflects upon them to establish authorial stance.	5–6
● Text is carefully written and form matches purpose, and interest of reader, so achieving its aim. Stylistic effects and relevant details are used confidently to achieve required viewpoint. Writer is aware of how to balance information, description and explanation.	7–8

Answers to Test Paper 1: School

Questions 1–7 are about *Roaring Boys*

1 Select and copy the words to show how the teacher knew how to find the room. **(1 mark)**
Focus: Describe, select and retrieve information and events or ideas from the text. Use quotation and reference to the text.
'The room was easily traced by the noise that was coming from it.'

2 Find and copy three things the teacher noticed as he came into the class. **(2 marks)**
Focus: Describe, select and retrieve information and events or ideas from the text. Use quotation and reference to the text.
Any two from: 'Enormous boys were everywhere doing indefensible things', 'A certain amount of furniture … doll's house things that rested on mountainous knees and swayed from side to side', 'One would, from time to time, crash to the floor', 'There were certainly fights going on', 'One desk was chasing another', 'The air was full of pieces of chalk'.

3 'If you don't shut up, I'll …'. What is the author's purpose in putting the three dots? **(3 marks)**
Focus: Deduce, infer and interpret information and events or ideas from the text.
The three dots indicate to the reader that the narrator's voice trailed off and that there was sudden silence. The teacher was using the statement but could not think of a suitable punishment or threat which would work on the boys. He knew that if he said something he must carry this out and he was afraid of failure.

The boys were also waiting for this threat. The statement silenced them for a while as they waited for the challenge. No teacher had been successful with them in the past and they were waiting to see what the next threat could be. The problem for the teacher was that he had to think of a threat which would be treated seriously by the pupils but also one which he could carry out successfully.

4 Quote two examples of the writer's use of description which give us a sense of the boys' rebelliousness. **(2 marks)**
Focus: Describe, select and retrieve information and events or ideas from the text. Use quotation and reference to the text.
Any two from: 'Enormous boys were everywhere doing indefensible things', 'One boy leaned back in his desk, indolently far back', 'He looked around and laughed' 'And, in falsetto, "Tell us a fairy story!"', 'My own accent came at me, insolently and indeed, most skilfully exaggerated'.

5 Explain why the 'studious-looking boy' 'hurt' the author. Look at what he does and what he represents. **(2 marks)**
Focus: Deduce, infer and interpret information and events or ideas from the text.
He is the one boy in the class who is not acting in a rebellious manner. He seems to act in judgement on the new teacher by raising his eyebrows and so makes the narrator feel even more of a failure.

The boy was reading, ignoring what was going on as if he had given up on the idea that any teacher could control the class and teach them anything.

6 The author asks a series of questions: 'Was I not a teacher? Had I not been approved by the Ministry itself? Was I really so puny, so ineffective?' They are rhetorical questions. What is the effect of these? **(2 marks)**
Focus: Comment on the writer's use of language, grammatical and literary features at word and sentence level.
Rhetorical questions do not require an answer. The author poses these questions to himself to assert his role. Unfortunately he cannot live up to this role so the effect is that the answers he would get would be negative.

7 The author wants us to be sympathetic towards him and not towards the pupils. Does he succeed? **(4 marks)**
Focus: Identify and comment on the writer's purposes and viewpoints, and the effect of the text on the reader.
In a sense the reader does not sympathise with the new teacher as he obviously has no understanding of the needs of the class in front of him (he is trying to teach them Chaucer). He has expectations that, just because he is a teacher, he deserves to be listened to (he says to himself, 'Had I not been approved by the Ministry itself?'). The humour created in the passage through the boys' bad behaviour also works against him. We tend to sympathise with the boys.

His language is fairly sophisticated compared to that of the boys, so it is unlikely that they would ever be able to understand one another. The boys are much more realistic in their approach and we are not surprised by what they say or do; in a sense we feel that the new teacher deserves it. As readers we would expect the teacher to be much more responsive to the needs of the class, but we feel some sympathy for him because he is being treated very badly by the boys.

Questions 8–15 are about *First Day at School*

8 Copy and complete the chart to show what the poem tells us. **(2 marks)**
Focus: Comment on the structure and organisation of texts, grammatical and presentational features at text level.

Setting	*A school playground*
Narrator	*A young child*
Other characters	*Other children*
Situation	*His or her first day at school*

9 Say what you think are the subjects of each of the three verses. Select and copy words to support what you say. **(2 marks)**
Focus: Comment on the structure and organisation of texts, grammatical and presentational features at text level.

Verse	Subjects	Quotation
1	*Child in playground watching others play*	*'Other children…', '…lived all their lives in playgrounds …', '…inventing games …'*
2	*The playground and how it keeps you in for 'lessins'*	*'Railings …', '…to keep out …', '…running away from the lessins'*
3	*Child worrying about what is expected of him or her – feeling confused – confusing the purpose of a teacher and so not really understanding why he or she is at school*	*'I wish I could remember my name …', '… mummy said…', '….tea-cher, the one who makes the tea'*

10 What do you find strange about the language used in the first line of the poem? **(1 mark)**
Focus: Deduce, infer and interpret information and events or ideas from the text.
The author uses the strange word 'millionbillionwillion'. This is a made-up word, one which would be used by a very small child to express just how far he or she felt away from the security of home.

11 Copy the chart and place a cross in the four boxes which tell us what the child noticed. **(2 marks)**
Focus: Describe, select and retrieve information and events or ideas from the text. Use quotation and reference to the text.

Noisy children	x	Children playing games	x
Children wearing wellingtons		Children who are much larger than himself	x
Children not wearing uniform		Quiet children	
Puddles in the playground		The school fence	x

12 Explain the following metaphor and its effect: 'Games / that are rough, that swallow you up.' **(2 marks)**
Focus: Comment on the writer's use of language, grammatical and literary features at word and sentence level.
The games in the playground are dangerous and the child imagines them to be like a monster. It is an image of fear. The image creates a picture of a crowded playground where the children disappear into crowds and never appear again, as if they have been swallowed.

13 Humour in the poem is created by the confusion of the child over the meaning of words. Select and copy two examples of this. Explain the confusion. **(3 marks)**
Focus: Describe, select and retrieve information and events or ideas from the text. Use quotation and reference to the text.
Any two of the following examples:
'Lessin': the child does not understand what a lesson is and only understands how it is pronounced. He or she thinks the word sounds 'small and slimy' like a creature.
'Glassrooms': again a mispronunciation, this time of 'classrooms'. Humour comes from the word-play on 'class' and 'glass', and the child's attempt to make sense of a new word by linking it to something he knows.
'Tea-cher': the child does not understand the concept of someone who teaches, so links the word with 'tea'. The humour comes from pupils studying the poem in class with the 'one who makes the tea' in front of them. It seems to deflate the air of authority which often surrounds teachers.

14 Select and copy two examples of statements in the poem which are not complete sentences. Why does the poet do this? What effect does the poet want these to create? Write the statements as complete sentences. Comment on the difference of effect. **(3 marks)**
Focus: Comment on the writer's use of language, grammatical and literary features at word and sentence level.
'So noisy?', 'So much at home they must have been born in uniform'.
There are many examples of statements which are not sentences. This is done purposely because the poet wishes to create the language of a young child and such children do not always use correct grammar. When you insert subjects and missing words (for example, 'Why are they so noisy? They are so much at home they must have been born in uniform') the sense of the young child disappears.

15 Explain how the writer communicates the point of view of a child in this poem. **(5 marks)**
Focus: Identify and comment on the writer's purposes and viewpoints, and the effect of the text on the reader.
The child has unconventional attitudes towards school and teachers because he or she does not understand the purpose of school (see above). This makes us feel sorry for the child because we get a greater sense of the child being at a loss, alone in the playground surrounded by a much noisier and larger world than that which he or she has been used to.

Questions 16–21 are about *Education in Scotland*

16 Find and copy four reasons from the first paragraph to say why education is important. **(2 marks)**
Focus: Describe, select and retrieve information and events or ideas from the text. Use quotation and reference to the text.
'To support and encourage children and young people to help them to live a happy and healthy life', 'To help them to develop and achieve their ambitions', 'To prepare them for a creative and productive working life', 'To prepare them to be citizens of a changing world'.

17 In the 'When?' section there are three paragraphs. Each paragraph covers a different topic. Copy the chart and draw a line to match each paragraph to its topic. **(2 marks)**
Focus: Describe, select and retrieve information and events or ideas from the text. Use quotation and reference to the text.

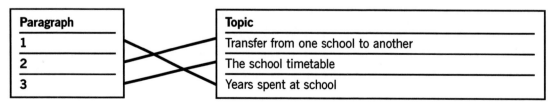

Paragraph		Topic
1		Transfer from one school to another
2		The school timetable
3		Years spent at school

18 Explain what the author means by: 'Different people are talented in different ways, whether that be in traditional academic areas, in practical vocational skills, or in other personal achievements.' **(2 marks)**
Focus: Comment on the writer's use of language, grammatical and literary features at word and sentence level.
The writer asserts that pupils can be successful according to the particular skills they have:
- *academic – by learning about more traditional school subjects*
- *practical vocational – by being creative and making things and by being good at things which will be useful in a future job*
- *other personal achievements – by developing personal skills and characteristics.*

19 The writer uses a metaphor: 'The school can be an oasis'. Explain the comparison and comment on how well you think it works in the description. **(2 marks)**
Focus: Comment on the writer's use of language, grammatical and literary features at word and sentence level.
The writer wants to communicate that the school provides what pupils need for their education. He does this by comparing the school to a fertile place. An oasis provides food and water – both vital for existence – in a desert. It is also an attractive place – a place in which travellers take pleasure. A school portrayed as an oasis could be said to provide pupils with something which is vital for life.

20 Suggest what the author might mean by the following statement. Give some examples of the 'other things'. 'Other things might take place in a school which specifically help with a young person's development. In the long-term future, the way in which schools are organised and managed might look different from today ...' **(2 marks)**

Focus: Deduce, infer and interpret information and events or ideas from the text.
The writer wishes to help us to understand that schools and education are changing as the world around us changes. We tend to think of school as being about 'lessons' in 'particular subjects' but the writer suggests that more important things can go on in school. We all have personal development to consider, so making friends and learning how to behave in certain circumstances is a skill not necessarily taught by learning about English or maths. Because of the changes in technology, it may be possible that the day will be organised differently. We may not have to come into a central place to be taught for certain hours every day. We could have 'anytime, anywhere' learning using computers and the Internet.

21 Explain the difference in use between the following uses of dashes and hyphens. **(4 marks)**
Focus: Comment on the writer's use of language, grammatical and literary features at word and sentence level.

There are places to learn other than schools – in libraries, colleges and universities, at work, in the community, or at home. These locations could help with teaching some subjects and skills more effectively – and there will be different people, as well as teachers, who can help deliver education.	*These are dashes – they separate ideas and allow them to be explained.*
The transfers from pre-school to primary school ... Providing a safe, purpose-built and stimulating environment is important ...	*These are hyphens – they join together words and ideas to make compound words.*

Answers: Test Paper 1

Test Paper 1 Mark scheme: Questions and assessment focuses

Question	Focus and number of marks (G: includes a focus on grammar)				
	Describe, select and retrieve information and events or ideas from the text. Use quotation and reference to the text.	Deduce, infer and interpret information and events or ideas from the text.	Comment on the structure and organisation of texts, grammatical and presentational features at text level.	Comment on the writer's use of language, grammatical and literary features at word and sentence level.	Identify and comment on the writer's purposes and viewpoints, and the effect of the text on the reader.
1:1	1				
1:2	2				
1:3		3			
1:4	2				
1:5		2			
1:6				2 G	
1:7					4
2:8			2		
2:9			2		
2:10		1			
2:11	2				
2:12				2	
2:13	3				
2:14				3 G	
2:15					5
3:16	2				
3:17	2				
3:18				2 G	
3:19				2	
3:20		2			
3:21				4 G	
Total	**14**	**8**	**4**	**15**	**9**

Answers to Test Paper 2: Monsters

Questions 1–7 are about *Dragon Slayer*

1 Copy and complete the chart to show what basic information the story gives you. **(1 mark)**
Focus: Describe, select and retrieve information and events or ideas from the text. Use quotation and reference to the text.

Setting Time of day Season	*Heorot – the Hall* *'night'* *spring*

2 Explain why Grendel the monster was angry at the door of Heorot. What does this show about his view of himself? **(2 marks)**
Focus: Deduce, infer and interpret information and events or ideas from the text.
The door of the hall was locked. This 'had stood unlatched for him so long'. He was used to coming into the hall and being in control. The door being closed was a sign that he was no longer important and so powerful. This is a sign that Beowulf will gain power.

3 Select and copy the two things which were uppermost in Grendel's mind when he was grasped by Beowulf. **(2 marks)**

Focus: Describe, select and retrieve information and events or ideas from the text. Use quotation and reference to the text.
He felt fear for the first time – 'for the first time he who had brought fear to so many caught the taste of it himself'. Beowulf's grip was so strong he knew he had met his match. He thought 'only of breaking the terrible hold upon his arm and flying back into the night' – running away.

4 The following are the subjects of the six paragraphs. Copy the boxes and write the appropriate letter in the correct box to show the structure of the passage. **(3 marks)**
Focus: Comment on the structure and organisation of texts, grammatical and presentational features at text level.
A. The monster flees, leaving a limb behind.
B. Beowulf fights Grendel.
C. Grendel approaches and breaks down the door of the Hall.
D. Beowulf's friends try to help.
E. Grendel kills Hondscio but Beowulf attacks.
F. The monster enters the Hall.

1	2	3	4	5	6
C	F	E	B	D	A

5 The writer uses very accurate and effective verbs, for example: 'Beowulf's hold was as fierce as ever; yet none the less the two figures **burst** apart – and Grendel with a frightful shriek **staggered** to the doorway and through it, and **fled wailing** into the night …'
This could be re-written as: 'Beowulf's hold was as fierce as ever; yet none the less the two figures **moved** apart – and Grendel with a frightful shriek **ran** to the doorway and through it, and **left complaining** into the night …'
Explain why the first version is better and what the verbs add to the effect of the writing. **(3 marks)**
Focus: Comment on the writer's use of language, grammatical and literary features at word and sentence level.
The verb 'burst' suggests the strength which lies behind it. 'Staggered' is a particular way of moving – it suggests the person is unsteady on his feet; 'fled' means running away in panic or in fear and the sound he makes is also one of fear. The verbs add to the picture of the defeat of the monster and therefore reflect on the heroism of Beowulf.

6 Find information in the passage to suggest that Beowulf is a hero. **(2 marks)**
Focus: Deduce, infer and interpret information and events or ideas from the text.
Right from the start he 'springs' up and faces the monster – he does not run away. Beowulf's grip is described as bringing fear to the monster, so he has superhuman strength – 'the strength of thirty men'. He fights directly and fearlessly with Grendel, and the creature knows that he has met his match – he makes various noises, those of 'a wild animal trapped'. Beowulf 'fought in silence'. He is described as the 'leader' of the men. Beowulf is so brave and strong that he tears the arm off the creature, which runs away in terror.

7 The passage aims to create a picture of a monster. How effective do you think the author has been? **(4 marks)**
Focus: Identify and comment on the writer's purposes and viewpoints, and the effect of the text on the reader.
The monster is associated with the dark from the start of the passage. He has obviously been used to being unchallenged by men because he is angry at finding the door of the hall locked.
Grendel is large and casts a 'monstrous shadow'. He is associated with death – even his eyes shed a 'ghastly corpse-light'. He is violent and bloodthirsty – 'snarling in rage', 'burst them in', 'tore him limb from limb and drank the warm blood'.
All of the author's language is extreme – the verbs are strong and violent, the adjectives adding to the frightful picture.

Questions 8–14 are about the *Loch Ness Monster*

8 Copy and complete the chart to say what each paragraph is about and how it is written. **(3 marks)**
Focus: Comment on the structure and organisation of texts, grammatical and presentational features at text level.

Paragraph	What it is about	Person	Tense	Reason
1	First appearances in 1933	1st and 3rd	Present and past	Author narrating and commenting on the past
2	Gould's book	1st and 3rd	Present and past	Author narrating and commenting on the past
3	Mr and Mrs Spicer's description	3rd	Past	Describing what had been
4	Mr Grant's description	3rd	Past	Describing what had been
5	Author's opinion	3rd	Past	Describes what it was

9 Find and copy information to explain why people offered rewards after the sighting of the monster. **(1 mark)**
Focus: Describe, select and retrieve information and events or ideas from the text. Use quotation and reference to the text.
'Mr Bertram Mills offered £20,000 to anyone who would deliver the monster alive to his circus, while the New York Zoological Society soon put up £5,000 as a similar inducement.' Both these groups wanted to display the creature in a circus or a zoo.

10 How do you know that the Loch Ness monster had become an 'international sensation'? **(2 marks)**
Focus: Deduce, infer and interpret information and events or ideas from the text.
You can tell there was international interest because representatives from the Japanese press were there and the New York Zoo was interested in capturing the creature.

11 Summarise the information you are given about Mr and Mrs Spicer's and Mr Grant's sightings of the Loch Ness monster. **(3 marks)**
Focus: Describe, select and retrieve information and events or ideas from the text. Use quotation and reference to the text.

	Mr and Mrs Spicer	**Mr Grant**
Size	*No information*	*About 18 feet long*
Shape	*Thick body, no legs, long neck*	*Front flippers and rounded tail*
Colour	*Grey*	*Black*
Movement	*Undulating, moved in a series of jerks*	*Arched its back on front and hind flippers alternately*
Head	*Not observed*	*Like an eel, large eyes*

12 Find and copy the words from paragraph 2 which show that the author has some admiration for Gould's book, but that he does not believe what it told him. **(2 marks)**
Focus: Describe, select and retrieve information and events or ideas from the text. Use quotation and reference to the text.
Gould's book was 'painstakingly compiled', which suggests he admired the work which had gone into it, but 'extremely unconvincing', which suggests that he did not believe what it contained.

13 Look carefully at the use of quotation marks in the following two examples. Explain the writer's differing purposes in using them. **(3 marks)**

> One enthusiast even offered, in the columns of the *Glasgow News*, to swim across the loch, 'as a challenge to the monster'…
> It had a thick body without any sign of legs, and a long neck which undulated up and down 'in the manner of a scenic railway'.

Focus: Comment on the writer's use of language, grammatical and literary features at word and sentence level.
In the first example, the author is quoting the words of the newspaper – something which has been written.
In the second example he is quoting the actual words of the speaker to illustrate the point.

14 Comment on the writer's attitude to the Loch Ness monster and how he communicates this in the writing. **(4 marks)**
Focus: Identify and comment on the writer's purposes and viewpoints, and the effect of the text on the reader.
The writer tries to give a fair account of the various sightings, although it is clear from the start – 'the most suspect' – that he is not a believer. He makes much of the joke of the spoof in the early paragraphs to show the kind of things people will do.
He is quite specific about the details of the two sightings and almost sounds excited by the details. It is obvious that he thinks these people have seen something but that it is not a monster.
He puts forward his own theory in the final paragraph. He gives reasons as to why people could be mistaken: for example, 'tricks of light'.

Questions 15–22 are about *The Kraken*

15 Select and copy words from the poem to prove that the poet imagines the monster to be at the bottom of the sea. **(1 mark)**
Focus: Describe, select and retrieve information and events or ideas from the text. Use quotation and reference to the text.
'Below the thunders of the upper deep.'

16 What does the word 'thunders' suggest about what it was like in this environment? **(2 marks)**
Focus: Deduce, infer and interpret information and events or ideas from the text.
'Thunders' suggests the noise of a large storm. This gives an impression of the noisy sea, the crashing waves and so on – but only at the surface. Below, all is quiet and mysterious while the monster sleeps.

Answers: Test Paper 2

17 Suggest a reason why the poet should decide to repeat the word 'far' in 'Far, far beneath in the abysmal sea'.
(1 mark)
Focus: Comment on the writer's use of language, grammatical and literary features at word and sentence level.
Repetition reinforces the idea. In this case, the author is trying to give a sense of just how deep the water is. He makes the reader say the word 'far' twice to make the idea of depth stronger.

18 The poet shows us a world of movement and life surrounding this sleeping monster. Find and copy two pieces of evidence to support this.
(2 marks)
Focus: Describe, select and retrieve information and events or ideas from the text. Use quotation and reference to the text.
The monster sleeps at the bottom of the sea. The light beams move – 'flee'; and the tentacles of the sea anemones drift around in the water – they 'winnow'.

19 What do the adjectives 'shadowy' and 'sickly' add to the effective description of the atmosphere under the sea in the following lines? '... faintest sunlights flee / About his shadowy sides ...' 'And far away into the sickly light ...'
(2 marks)
Focus: Comment on the writer's use of language, grammatical and literary features at word and sentence level.
The world under the sea will be dark. The poet is creating a picture of the underwater but very deep down – so deep that a monster can remain undiscovered for centuries. Only tiny amounts of light can penetrate the gloom – hence the 'shadowy' sides which suggest movement of the light by the water currents. The 'sickly' light shows us just how dim it is. The word is linked with illness and people who lack a healthy colour because they are sick.

20 The following lines describe the movements of undersea creatures: 'Unnumber'd and enormous polypi / Winnow with giant arms the slumbering green.' What impressions are created by the metaphors in them?
(3 marks)
Focus: Comment on the writer's use of language, grammatical and literary features at word and sentence level.
Winnowing is a gentle movement – being at the mercy of the wind. Hence the tentacles look as if they are being blown around here and there by the wind rather than by the water currents. The word almost sounds soft. This reinforces the picture of a silent world where things move in slow motion or not at all. Even the sea itself – 'the green' – is seen as sleeping.

21 The poem ends deliberately with a sound – 'roaring' – but the rest of the poem has given an impression of quietness. Why should this be?
(2 marks)
Focus: Identify and comment on the writer's purposes and viewpoints, and the effect of the text on the reader.
The legend of the Kraken says that one day, at the end of the world, it will awake to help in the destruction of the world. The word 'roaring' reminds us that although this world is silent now, the creature is just sleeping. This is the kind of noise it will make. It is the kind of threat which should lurk at the back of our minds.

22 The poet aims to create a mysterious atmosphere of a sleeping monster which will one day awake and destroy the world. How successful is he in this?
(2 marks)
Focus: Identify and comment on the writer's purposes and viewpoints, and the effect of the text on the reader.
This question brings together many of the points raised in the previous questions, for example:
- *the idea of the Kraken about to awake*
- *the silent, peaceful world it lives in now*
- *the hints at the end that it will awake and can destroy.*

Testing KS3 English Year 7 © Nelson Thornes 2003

Test Paper 2 Mark scheme: Questions and assessment focuses

Question	Focus and number of marks (G: includes a focus on grammar)				
	Describe, select and retrieve information and events or ideas from the text. Use quotation and reference to the text.	Deduce, infer and interpret information and events or ideas from the text.	Comment on the structure and organisation of texts, grammatical and presentational features at text level.	Comment on the writer's use of language, grammatical and literary features at word and sentence level.	Identify and comment on the writer's purposes and viewpoints, and the effect of the text on the reader.
1:1	1				
1:2		2			
1:3	2				
1:4			3		
1:5				3 G	
1:6		2			
1:7					4
2:8			3		
2:9	1				
2:10		2			
2:11	3				
2:12	2				
2:13				3 G	
2:14					4
3:15	1				
3:16		2			
3:17				1	
3:18	2				
3:19				2 G	
3:20				3	
3:21					2
3:22					2
Total	**12**	**8**	**6**	**12**	**12**

Answers to Test Paper 3: Times of celebration

Questions 1–8 are about *Christmas*

1 Find and copy three details from the text which explain why 'primitive farming peoples' needed a mid-winter celebration. **(1 mark)**
   Focus: Describe, select and retrieve information and events or ideas from the text. Use quotation and reference to the text.
   Life was very hard for these people. Winter was very cold. Their clothes and homes were inadequate. They would be lacking in food.

2 Explain why these people watched natural phenomena so intently. **(1 mark)**
   Focus: Deduce, infer and interpret information and events or ideas from the text.
   The sun, moon, stars, wind and rain were central to their lives because they governed what they did, what they ate and how they lived. They were seen as signs from the gods.

3 Copy and complete the following chart to summarise what the passage tells you about the origins of Christmas traditions. **(3 marks)**
   Focus: Describe, select and retrieve information and events or ideas from the text. Use quotation and reference to the text.

Tradition	Origin
Decorating with evergreens	*Would make things green more quickly in spring*
Candles	*Would strengthen the sun*
Christmas dinner	*Meal of the winter festival was the greatest meal of the year*
The Crib	*Made the Christmas story simple for those who could not read*
Boxing Day	*Apprentices collected money in boxes on this day*
Christmas trees	*From Germany – came with Prince Albert*

4 Match each of the first five paragraphs to its subject. **(3 marks)**
   Focus: Comment on the structure and organisation of texts, grammatical and presentational features at text level.

Paragraph 1	The need for celebration
Paragraph 2	The use of light and fire as symbols
Paragraph 3	The connection between Christmas and old traditions
Paragraph 4	The inspiration for food
Paragraph 5	The use of natural vegetation as a symbol

5 Explain in your own words what happened during Saturnalia and how it came to be incorporated into the celebration of Christmas. **(2 marks)**
   Focus: Deduce, infer and interpret information and events or ideas from the text.
   Saturnalia was the festival held 17–23 December. It was a festival of fun.
   Roles were reversed – the masters became servants and vice versa.
   All men should be equal.
   The Lord of Misrule could command anyone and everything.
   No one was to work.
   People were to be peaceful.

6   How did the concept of a winter celebration change after the Middle Ages?   **(1 mark)**
    Focus: Describe, select and retrieve information and events or ideas from the text. Use quotation and reference to the text.
    The Middle Ages brought Christianity and its Nativity story and this was mixed with the more pagan stories and traditions.

7   The writer uses italics and quotation marks for the following piece of text, as well as setting it out differently.
    Explain why.   **(2 marks)**

    > *'All business, public or private, is forbidden during the feast
    > days, except that which contributes to sport and revelry. Let no
    > one work except cooks and bakers.
    > All men shall be equal, free and slave, rich and poor. Anger
    > and threats are against the law.'*

    Focus: Comment on the writer's use of language, grammatical and literary features at word and sentence level.
    This quotation is obviously an original law of the time referring to the festival. The author is therefore quoting it (using quotation marks) and makes it look different from the rest of the text by putting it in italics and centring it on the page.

8   In the passage the author aims to inform the reader in an accurate and entertaining way. How successful is he
    in doing this?   **(3 marks)**
    Focus: Identify and comment on the writer's purposes and viewpoints, and the effect of the text on the reader.
    The author explains things clearly and logically and uses interesting examples to discuss the traditions of the festival – ones which we can understand: for example, the origins of stirring the Christmas pudding and of Boxing Day. He gives an impression of having researched the article and appears to know his material: for example, the law he quotes. He deals with the festival in a chronological way, so that we can see how the festival has developed over time.
    His tone is somewhat humorous, especially in the final section about Christmas cards.

Questions 9–16 are about *Plot Night*

9   Find and copy two pieces of information from the first two paragraphs which tell us that we are at a November
    5th celebration.   **(1 mark)**
    Focus: Describe, select and retrieve information and events or ideas from the text. Use quotation and reference to the text.
    'Carrying the guy' and 'a Roman candle was shooting up its fire'. Both of these are associated with November 5th celebrations.

10 Select and copy two pieces of evidence to show how Amy reacted to her first experience of fireworks. Explain
    why you have chosen each piece of evidence.   **(3 marks)**
    Focus: Describe, select and retrieve information and events or ideas from the text. Use quotation and reference to the text.
    Evidence: she jumped at all the bangs.
    Explanation: she did not realise that certain fireworks were meant to frighten people as well as to appear attractive.
    Evidence: when she saw the fountains she thought they were water.
    Explanation: Amy believed that the stream of fire coming from the firework was water because she had no concept of how fireworks looked.

11 The passage uses poetic language and devices to describe the fireworks. Explain the simile in: 'It was like a
    small sun flaming in the night'. Comment on how effective you think this is as an image for a firework.

    (2 marks)
    Focus: Comment on the writer's use of language, grammatical and literary features at word and sentence level.
    The poet wants to communicate the brightness of the firework. It is only small, so he compares it to 'a small sun', the brightest thing we know. It is made even brighter by the comparison of the light and the darkness at night.

12 In the following paragraph the author uses a special technique for making the fireworks come alive. What impressions does he create and how does the technique work?   **(3 marks)**

> Mary got by herself, and exploded her fireworks one by one until they were all gone. Then she picked up the bodies and threw them in the fire. One of them was still alive, and spat back a red blob, then a green blob, before wrinkling itself up black in the embers.

Focus: Comment on the writer's use of language, grammatical and literary features at word and sentence level.
The writer uses personification. The spent cartridges of the fireworks are imagined as 'dead' – of no more use – and are therefore described as 'bodies'. The actions of the fireworks when lit are compared to a human being. One of them explodes; this makes Mary imagine that it is spitting back at her. Later in the sentence it is seen as controlling its own movement and so having a mind of its own like a human – 'wrinkling itself up'. The imagery makes the scene much more active and lively.

13 Explain why the writer chose to repeat a word in the following description: 'Then there was a shower of new bright stars in the sky, dropping, dropping, with smoke above them, and fading as they came'.   **(1 mark)**
Focus: Identify and comment on the writer's purposes and viewpoints, and the effect of the text on the reader.
The writer is describing how the sparks of the firework fall to earth after the explosion. The children want the pretty sight to last forever as they watch the sparks slowly fall to earth. To make the process seem even longer the writer repeats the word 'dropping'. We have to say it twice and the shape of the word makes us say it slowly, so it really does prolong the experience.

14 Write about the difficulties of finding an appropriate place to launch the rocket. Why was the final place they chose a suitable one?   **(3 marks)**
Focus: Deduce, infer and interpret information and events or ideas from the text.
The rocket was so big that it could not be stood in a bottle for lighting. There was a risk of it toppling over and shooting off horizontally, causing damage. They found a hollow gatepost in the park. Presumably this was long and deep enough to support the stick of the rocket. It was partially filled with stones, put there over the years by people in the park. It was coincidentally exactly the right length.

15 Place these statements about the final rocket and its effect in the correct order. Copy the boxes and write the appropriate letter in the correct box.   **(3 marks)**
    A. It curved and exploded before disappearing.
    B. The children heard the used rocket dropping in the park.
    C. Once lit, it glowed and made some noise but did not seem to move.
    D. The lights went out and there was silence.
    E. It made a loud noise and went up into the sky.
    F. Then it exploded again into a shower of bright lights which streamed downwards.
Focus: Comment on the structure and organisation of texts, grammatical and presentational features at text level.

1	2	3	4	5	6
C	E	A	D	F	B

16 What evidence can you find to suggest that this passage is taken from a book meant for younger children?
                                                                                                          (3 marks)

Focus: Identify and comment on the writer's purposes and viewpoints, and the effect of the text on the reader.
There are many examples which show that this comes from a book written for children.
The subject matter is very exciting to children and the characters in the story are excited by the fireworks. Young children need shorter sentences in their writing because they cannot read very well. There are many examples of this. The language and vocabulary are fairly simple.
The children call their parents 'mummy and daddy'.
There appears to be a gang at the heart of the story – 'L for Leader' – and this would appeal to children.
The tone of the passage communicates the excitement and explains things carefully and simply.

Questions 17–23 are about *Diwali in Kerala*

17 Find and copy two pieces of information which give the reader a sense of time of day and location.   **(2 marks)**
    Focus: Describe, select and retrieve information and events or ideas from the text. Use quotation and reference to the text.
    'Fading light' and 'pivotal moment of dusk' tell us what time of day we are considering.
    'Over the palms' suggests an exotic location.

18 Explain why the birds are 'in silhouette'.   **(1 mark)**
    Focus: Deduce, infer and interpret information and events or ideas from the text.
    The light is fading. It is dusk. There would be no bright lights here. The narrator is watching and can only see the dark outlines of the birds, so he thinks of them as 'silhouettes'.

19 According to the legend, the King of the Monkeys helped Rama to cross the sea. From the information given in the poem, outline how you think they did this.   **(2 marks)**
    Focus: Deduce, infer and interpret information and events or ideas from the text.
    The poem tells us, 'Cleverly, the King of the Monkeys and his army have knitted their tails / Across the blockage of ocean to Sri Lanka'.
    This would suggest that the monkeys linked their tails to form a kind of bridge across the sea. In this way the 'blockage' was overcome and Rama was able to cross the sea and rescue his wife Sita.

20 Explain the metaphors in the following two examples. Describe the picture they create in your mind:
    'the weaponry of fireworks', 'in a multi-coloured carnage'.   **(4 marks)**
    Focus: Comment on the writer's use of language, grammatical and literary features at word and sentence level.
    Metaphors are comparisons and so the first thing to do is to look closely at the points of comparison.
    'Fireworks' are compared to 'weapons' – things which are used in wars. The associations are bright noises, loud bangs and danger. In this case it is a suitable image because the purpose of the fireworks is to destroy evil – in the form of Ravana, the King of the Demons.
    The fireworks explode in a 'carnage' – wholesale slaughter. The colours in the sky emerge in a sudden explosion of many colours and shapes and then disappear very quickly. The evil has been destroyed in this act of 'carnage' but in fact the fireworks do not do anybody any harm.

21 'The body of evil must be reduced to dust.' From the evidence in the poem about the meaning of Diwali, what do the exploding fireworks symbolise?   **(1 mark)**
    Focus: Deduce, infer and interpret information and events or ideas from the text.
    The people know that Ravana (evil) has been destroyed by Rama but, to make sure, every year the fireworks become a symbol of their own destruction of evil. By making the noise and destroying the fireworks they are destroying the King of the Demons again.

22 Explain why the author has pictured Rama smiling. How does this link with the following lines?
    'But this is not an end, just the beginning … / … He knows that light will always struggle to shine through darkness'.   **(2 marks)**
    Focus: Deduce, infer and interpret information and events or ideas from the text.
    Statues of Rama are normally shown smiling. In this case the author is suggesting that the god is pleased that evil has been destroyed again. The end of evil is the chance to start being good. The god is smiling because he knows that good will always overcome evil: light will always overcome darkness – which is the meaning of the festival.

23 The poet aims to give you an atmospheric description of a festival and its effect on the narrator. How successful has he been?   **(3 marks)**
    Focus: Identify and comment on the writer's purposes and viewpoints, and the effect of the text on the reader.
    The poem starts in a silent, thoughtful mood, moves through noise and bright colours – almost violence – and ends again in 'silence and faded light'. In this way the poet has created a structure which recreates the festival itself.
    The pupils will already have considered some of the imagery of the poem and why it is effective and what the festival really means in their answers to earlier questions.

Answers: Test Paper 3

Test Paper 3 Mark scheme: Questions and assessment focuses

Question	Describe, select and retrieve information and events or ideas from the text. Use quotation and reference to the text.	Deduce, infer and interpret information and events or ideas from the text.	Comment on the structure and organisation of texts, grammatical and presentational features at text level.	Comment on the writer's use of language, grammatical and literary features at word and sentence level.	Identify and comment on the writer's purposes and viewpoints, and the effect of the text on the reader.
	Focus and number of marks (G: includes a focus on grammar)				
1:1	1				
1:2		1			
1:3	3				
1:4			3		
1:5		2			
1:6	1				
1:7				2 G	
1:8					3
2:9	1				
2:10	3				
2:11				2 G	
2:12				3 G	
2:13					1
2:14		3			
2:15			3		
2:16					3
3:17	2				
3:18		1			
3:19		2			
3:20				4 G	
3:21		1			
3:22		2			
3:23					3
Total	11	12	6	11	10

Testing KS3 English Year 7 © Nelson Thornes 2003

Answers to Test Paper 4: Woodlands

Questions 1–7 are about *The Wind in the Willows*

1   Select and copy the words from the first paragraph which show what the weather was like.   **(1 mark)**
   Focus: Describe, select and retrieve information and events or ideas from the text. Use quotation and reference to the text.
   'cold', 'hard steely sky'.

2   Find and copy three phrases which tell you what time of year it was.   **(2 marks)**
   Focus: Describe, select and retrieve information and events or ideas from the text. Use quotation and reference to the text.
   'The country lay bare and lifeless', 'winter day', 'Nature was deep in her annual slumber'.

3   What is the purpose of the dashes in the following sentence? 'He passed another hole, and another, and another; and then – yes! – no! – yes! certainly a little narrow face, with hard eyes, had flashed up for an instant from a hole, and was gone.'
   Focus: Comment on the writer's use of language, grammatical and literary features at word and sentence level.
   The dashes indicate the Mole's hesitation, stopping and starting in fear and turning to see what was behind him. They create the effect of fear or apprehension. The writer creates this effect to show how the Mole feels about going into the Wild Wood and to build up tension.

4   Quote two examples of the writer's use of contrast which emphasise the coldness and bareness of the Wild Wood.   **(2 marks)**
   Focus: Describe, select and retrieve information and events or ideas from the text. Use quotation and reference to the text.
   'cold still afternoon' and 'warm parlour', 'shabby poverty' and 'riot in rich masquerade'.

5   How did the Mole feel about the Wild Wood when he first thought about it?   **(2 marks)**
   Focus: Deduce, infer and interpret information and events or ideas from the text.
   He felt cheerful and eager to reach the Wild Wood ('with great cheerfulness of spirit he pushed on towards the Wild Wood').

6   What is the first suggestion that the Wild Wood is not a pleasant place?   **(2 marks)**
   Focus: Deduce, infer and interpret information and events or ideas from the text.
   The Wild Wood is described as 'low and threatening'; this contrasts with the Mole's first thoughts about it, when he approached it with great cheerfulness.

7   How does the writer gradually build up the threatening atmosphere of the Wild Wood?   **(4 marks)**
   Focus: Identify and comment on the writer's purposes and viewpoints, and the effect of the text on the reader.
   The words 'There was nothing to alarm him at first entry' suggest that something is going to alarm the Mole, following the previous description of the Wild Wood ('low and threatening'). They prepare the reader for the threatening atmosphere of the wood.
   Soon the things around the Mole take on threatening appearances: the writer uses comparisons such as 'funguses on stumps resembled caricatures' and metaphors such as 'holes made ugly mouths at him'. The atmosphere of the Wild Wood is built up through the device of making readers feel as if they are following the Mole into the Wood, and stopping and starting with him as things appear and disappear: for example, 'a little narrow face' which 'flashed up for an instant', the 'little, evil, wedge-shaped face' which he thought he saw for an instant and the hundreds of faces which seemed to come and go rapidly.
   Three short paragraphs consisting of one sentence each mirror one another, adding to the effect: 'Then the faces began', 'Then the whistling began' and 'Then the pattering began'.

Questions 8–15 are about *The Way Through the Woods*

8   Find and copy three examples of animals which live in the woods.   **(2 marks)**
   Focus: Describe, select and retrieve information and events or ideas from the text. Use quotation and reference to the text.
   Any three from: 'ring-dove', 'badger', 'otter', 'trout', 'horse'.

9 How have the woods changed? Select and copy words to support what you say. **(2 marks)**
   Focus: **Deduce, infer and interpret information and events or ideas from the text.**
   There used to be a road through the woods, but it has been closed ('They shut the road through the woods',
   'There was once a road through the woods').

10 What is the effect of the phrase 'misty solitudes' in the second verse? **(1 mark)**
   Focus: **Comment on the writer's use of language, grammatical and literary features at word and sentence level.**
   This phrase suggests quietness and loneliness, but not peacefulness: it has a ghostly effect, especially as it
   follows the reference to horses cantering along the road through the woods. It is as if there were a ghostly
   horse being ridden along the old road through the woods.

11 Find two examples of internal rhyme in the second verse. **(2 marks)**
   Focus: **Comment on the writer's use of language, grammatical and literary features at word and sentence level.**
   'The night air cools on the trout-ringed pools' and 'You will hear the beat of a horse's feet'.

12 How does the poet suggest that, although 'you would never know / There was once a road through the woods',
   the road has not completely disappeared? **(3 marks)**
   Focus: **Identify and comment on the writer's purposes and viewpoints, and the effect of the text on the reader.**
   It is as if the actions of people (closing the road) could not completely eradicate the road; it would not go
   away and a trace of it remained: 'It is [not was] under the coppice and heath' and 'only the keeper' sees
   where it was. There is also a suggestion that the ghosts of past travellers along the road continue to use it:
   the poet describes a horse which can be heard 'steadily cantering through' the woods.

13 Which two lines in the first verse create an atmosphere of peace and tranquillity, and how does the poet use
   alliteration to create this effect? **(3 marks)**
   Focus: **Identify and comment on the writer's purposes and viewpoints, and the effect of the text on the reader.**
   The words 'ring-dove broods' and 'badgers roll at ease' suggest peace and tranquillity. The alliteration of 'r'
   sounds creates a gentle effect.

14 Describe the atmosphere of the second verse. Which words create this effect? **(3 marks)**
   Focus: **Identify and comment on the writer's purposes and viewpoints, and the effect of the text on the reader.**
   The second verse, like the first one, is very still and quiet, but it also has a ghostly atmosphere. It is as if the
   horse which can be heard cantering along the road is a ghostly traveller from the past. The alliteration of 's'
   sounds helps to create a whispering effect which adds to the ghostly atmosphere: 'whistles his mate', 'swish
   of a skirt' and 'misty solitudes'.

15 What is the effect of repetition in the poem? **(4 marks)**
   Focus: **Identify and comment on the writer's purposes and viewpoints, and the effect of the text on the reader.**
   Any effect which is justified by reference to the poem should be accepted. The most noticeable repetition is:
   'They shut the road through the woods' and 'There was once a road through the woods'. This repetition
   emphasises that, even though the keeper can still see the old road, it is closed; visitors nowadays cannot see
   it. The repetition of the rhythm of these lines in the last line of the poem ('But there is no road through the
   woods') emphasises that the road was closed; however, the addition of the word 'but' suggests a doubt about
   the finality of the closure (they closed the road, but you can still hear horses cantering along it).

Questions 16–21 are about *Britain's rainforests need protecting now*

16 Find and copy from the second paragraph the four aspects of climate change which affect the survival of
   Britain's ancient woodland. **(2 marks)**
   Focus: **Describe, select and retrieve information and events or ideas from the text. Use quotation and reference to the text.**
   'higher temperatures', 'changes in rainfall patterns', 'drought', 'the frequency of storms'.

17 Explain what 'hangs in the balance' means in the first paragraph. **(1 mark)**
Focus: Comment on the writer's use of language, grammatical and literary features at word and sentence level.
'Hangs in the balance' is a metaphor which suggests that the survival of woodlands is in a precarious position. It is as if the balance (a pair of scales) could be tipped in either direction if some quite small event were to alter the present situation.

18 Three 'key factors' are mentioned in the report as causing the future of ancient woodlands to 'hang in the balance'. Each factor is the topic of a paragraph. Match each paragraph to its topic. **(2 marks)**
Focus: Comment on the structure and organisation of texts, grammatical and presentational features at text level.

Paragraph		Topic
2		Damage by animals and by other types of trees
3		Changes in climate
4		A lack of legal protection

(Paragraph 2 → Changes in climate; Paragraph 3 → A lack of legal protection; Paragraph 4 → Damage by animals and by other types of trees)

19 Explain why bullets are used in the final paragraph of the report. **(2 marks)**
Focus: Comment on the structure and organisation of texts, grammatical and presentational features at text level.
The bullets separate and emphasise the four measures which the report recommends.

20 Copy and complete the table with information from the passage about the effects of different aspects of the 'key factors' (identified in question 18) on ancient woodlands. **(3 marks)**
Focus: Describe, select and retrieve information and events or ideas from the text. Use quotation and reference to the text.

Key factor	Effects on trees and other plants	Effects on animals
Mild winters	*Increasing numbers of insect pests*	*None described*
Droughts	*Make them vulnerable to disease*	*Make them vulnerable to disease*
Intensive farming	*Fragments of woodland become isolated*	*None described*
Overgrazing by livestock and deer	*Halts the growth of new trees. Prevents ancient woodland from regenerating*	*None described*
Dense plantations of conifers	*Ancient woodlands fight for survival beneath their dense canopies*	*None described*

21 This passage aims to persuade the government, and anyone who can influence the government, that ancient woodlands need to be protected. How successful is it? **(4 marks)**
Focus: Identify and comment on the writer's purposes and viewpoints, and the effect of the text on the reader.
The report is fairly successful in appealing to people's feelings about ancient woodlands through its use of language. The language includes expressive metaphors and figures of speech such as 'hangs in the balance' and 'fighting to survive'; strong verbs such as 'threatened' and 'destroyed'; and strong adjectives such as 'dramatic' and 'extinct'. There are opportunities to make more use of this type of expressive language: for example, 'particularly at risk' in paragraph 2 could be replaced by something more appealing to people's feelings, such as 'are threatened most of all with extinction'.

The report is fairly convincing because most of its statements are supported by facts: for example, the effects of climatic change are supported by examples, as is the effect of overgrazing by livestock and deer. However, there are places where it could be more specific: for example, the phrase 'are not helping' (referring to loopholes in the law) does not tell us in what way these loopholes are not helping.

Test Paper 4 Mark scheme: Questions and assessment focuses

Question	Focus and number of marks (G: includes a focus on grammar)				
	Describe, select and retrieve information and events or ideas from the text. Use quotation and reference to the text.	Deduce, infer and interpret information and events or ideas from the text.	Comment on the structure and organisation of texts, grammatical and presentational features at text level.	Comment on the writer's use of language, grammatical and literary features at word and sentence level.	Identify and comment on the writer's purposes and viewpoints, and the effect of the text on the reader.
1:1	1				
1:2	2				
1:3				3 G	
1:4	2				
1:5		2			
1:6		2			
1:7					4
2:8	2				
2:9		2			
2:10				1	
2:11				2	
2:12					3
2:13					3
2:14					3
2:15					4
3:16	2				
3:17				1	
3:18			2		
3:19			2 G		
3:20	3				
3:21					4
Total	12	6	4	7	21

Answers to Test Paper 5: Football

Questions 1–7 are about *A Legend in his Own Time*

1   The writer said that there were myths about Bill Shankly. Select and copy the three personal qualities which he called 'myths'.   **(1 mark)**
Focus: Describe, select and retrieve information and events or ideas from the text. Use quotation and reference to the text.
'tough', 'hard', 'ruthless'.

2   With what did the writer compare Bill Shankly in the second paragraph, and for what two reasons?   **(2 marks)**
Focus: Comment on the writer's use of language, including grammatical and literary features at word and sentence level.
The comparison which the writer made was 'he's like an old Collie dog'. The reason he made the comparison was to emphasise that Bill Shankly drove his players hard but he cared for them and would never say anything against them ('drive them, certainly, but bite them – never').

3   Find two other comparisons in the passage, and copy and complete the chart. Comment on the impression produced by the comparison.   **(3 marks)**
Focus: Comment on the writer's use of language, including grammatical and literary features at word and sentence level.

The thing, person or place compared	What he, she or it is compared with	The impression created
'great sides'	*waves on the seashore*	*the players in the team surging backwards and forward as one*
'nervous energy'	*electricity*	*great energy*

4   What, according to the writer, was the most important thing Bill Shankly did to make Liverpool a top-class football team?   **(2 marks)**
Focus: Deduce, infer and interpret information and events or ideas from the text.
He spoke about (and to) the teams as if there were no chance of another team beating them ('They have belief in one another'). He believed in people and inspired them ('He must be the greatest inspirer in the game', 'they didn't have a bad player in his side – according to him').

5   List three qualities which made Bill Shankly a great player when he was a footballer. Select and quote from the passage.   **(2 marks)**
Focus: Describe, select and retrieve information and events or ideas from the text. Use quotation and reference to the text.
Any three from: 'superbly fit', 'didn't know when he was licked', 'a good tackler', 'a brave player', 'straightforward', 'tough', 'with infectious enthusiasm'.

6   Look for a metaphor near the end of the passage and describe the impression it creates of Bill Shankly.
(2 marks)
Focus: Comment on the writer's use of language, including grammatical and literary features at word and sentence level.
The metaphor 'but of course he did light up the city and the game' gives the impression of someone who made a lasting impression on the world of football and changed it, in some way, for the better.

7   The writer aims to create a picture of someone special in the world of football. How successful is it?   **(4 marks)**
Focus: Identify and comment on the writer's purposes and viewpoints, and the effect of the text on the reader.
The writer creates the impression that Bill Shankly was someone special through the use of comparisons like 'He's like an old Collie dog', metaphors such as 'he did light up the city and the game', superlatives such as 'the most amazing thing', and 'the greatest inspirer', and intensified adjectives such as 'superbly fit'. The use of expressive figures of speech such as 'trying to condense an encyclopedia into a football programme' adds to this impression, as do strong adjectives such as 'wonderful', 'marvellous' and 'amazing'.

Answers: Test Paper 5

Questions 8–14 are about *A Perfect Match*

8   This is a narrative poem. How can you tell?   **(2 marks)**
    Focus: Comment on the structure and organisation of texts, grammatical and presentational features at text level.
    The use of the past tense shows that this is a narrative poem, as does the fact that it is a chronological recount: it traces the meeting of the two lovers, their conversation, the man's proposal of marriage, the wedding, the honeymoon and setting up home.

9   How is the love story linked with football throughout the poem?   **(2 marks)**
    Focus: Comment on the structure and organisation of texts, grammatical and presentational features at text level.
    There are word-plays on the names of football teams which create humour: for example, 'Is your Motherwell?' mentions the football club Motherwell and is used as a question 'Is your mother well?'. Other football terms are used such as 'Coca Cola Cup'.

10 Copy and complete the chart to show six other football clubs which are mentioned in the poem and explain the puns on their names.   **(3 marks)**
    Focus: Comment on the writer's use of language, grammatical and literary features at word and sentence level.

Name of football club	Similar sounding word or words with a different meaning
Alloa	Hello
Motherwell	mother well
Meadowbank	a meadow bank
Queen of the South	a pet name by which the man addresses the woman
Sheffield Wednesday	Sheffield on Wednesday
Accrington Stanley	Accrington (a town in Lancashire), Stanley (the man's name)
United	united (as a married couple)
Hearts	the lovers' hearts
Stirling	sterling (silver)
Forfar	from far (and wide)
Crewe	crew
Raith	raise
Ayr	air
Partick-ularly	particularly
Villa	villa (a house)
Walsall	walls all
Chesterfield	a chesterfield sofa

11 In verse 2, 'Academicals' refers to the Scottish football club Hamilton Academicals. The play on words here is not obvious; 'Academicals' is probably used as a slang or nonsense word for what?   **(2 marks)**
    Focus: Comment on the writer's use of language, including grammatical and literary features at word and sentence level.
    'Academicals' sounds like a slang word for being drunk. It suggests 'hiccups'.

12 Chesterfield is a football club. Reread verse 8. Why should people sit on a Chesterfield?   **(2 marks)**
    Focus: Deduce, infer and interpret information and events or ideas from the text.
    A chesterfield is a type of sofa.

13 Comment on the rhythm of the poem and how this suits its tone.   **(3 marks)**
    Focus: Comment on the structure and organisation of texts, grammatical and presentational features at text level.
    The rhythm is brisk and lively to match the light-hearted tone of the poem. The regular, repeated line lengths and rhyme pattern help to create this effect. The poem is split into eight verses, each with an identical pattern of alternating longer and shorter lines, with the second and fourth lines rhyming. The regular rhythm creates a sing-song effect, which also contributes to the light-hearted tone.

14 The poem is meant to be funny. How successful is it? **(4 marks)**
   Focus: Identify and comment on the writer's purposes and viewpoints, and the effect of the text on the reader.
   The use of puns and word-plays on the names of football clubs makes the poem humorous.
   The opening line sets this tone: 'We met in Nottingham Forest' (the name of a place near Nottingham as well as the name of a football club). The humorous tone is continued as pun after pun appears, sometimes achieved purely by the use of punctuation: for example, in 'Sheffield, Wednesday' and 'Accrington, Stanley'.
   The rhyme pattern (second and fourth lines of each verse) and the regular pattern of line lengths help to create a regular rhythm with a sing-song effect which contributes to the light-hearted tone of the poem.

Questions 15–22 are about *Magpies come from behind to beat Charlton*

15 Name another football team, apart from Charlton, which Newcastle had recently beaten and one which had defeated them. **(1 mark)**
   Focus: Describe, select and retrieve information and events or ideas from the text. Use quotation and reference to the text.
   Newcastle had recently beaten Sunderland and the Italian team Juventus (pupils should mention only one of these teams) and had been defeated by Blackburn Rovers.

16 If you did not know that the nickname of Newcastle United was 'the Magpies' and that their home ground was St James' Park, how could you find these out from the passage? Select and copy words from the passage which tell you about each of these. **(1 mark)**
   Focus: Describe, select and retrieve information and events or ideas from the text. Use quotation and reference to the text.
   The headline 'Magpies come from behind to defeat Charlton' tells the reader which football teams the report is about and the first sentence of the second paragraph reveals that 'Magpies' are Newcastle United:
   'Newcastle United boss Robson had to watch the entire 2–1 victory over Charlton Athletic …'
   The combination of three pieces of information from the passage makes it clear that St James' Park is the home ground of Newcastle United:
   The opening paragraph of the report begins 'Sir Bobby Robson was given the perfect pick-me-up at St James' Park …'. This tells readers that the match took place at St James' Park.
   We know that Newcastle won the match 2–1 ('Newcastle boss Robson had to watch the entire 2–1 victory over Charlton Athletic…').
   The score at the end of the report is given: ' 2–1'; since a home team's score is always given first, we know that the home team was Newcastle.

17 Name as many as you can of the players who were in the Newcastle United and Charlton Athletic teams for the match reported in the passage. Do not name players from any memories you might have of the match; select and copy the names only of players mentioned in the passage. Not all the players might be named. Copy and complete the chart. **(3 marks)**
   Focus: Describe, select and retrieve information and events or ideas from the text. Use quotation and reference to the text.

Newcastle United	Charlton Athletic
Shola Ameobi	*Dean Kiely*
Jermaine Jenas	*Richard Rufus*
Alan Shearer	*Gary Rowett*
Michael Chopra (substitute)	*Mark Fish*
Laurent Robert	*John Robinson*
Speed	*Shaun Bartlett*
Andy O'Brien	
Shay Given	
Andy Griffin	
Solano	
Titus Bramble	

18 Which players scored Newcastle United's two goals and who scored Charlton Athletic's goal? **(2 marks)**

Focus: Describe, select and retrieve information and events or ideas from the text. Use quotation and reference to the text.

Andy Griffin and Laurent Robert scored Newcastle United's goals: 'Andy Griffin continued his rise to hero status on Tyneside. Shearer rolled the ball to the on-rushing Griffin, who from 18 yards struck a sweet right foot shot that powered into Kiely's top corner' and 'Kiely had to be alert to save a low Robert drive nine minutes after the restart. But five minutes later the Irish goalkeeper could do nothing about the £10m man's left-foot bullet that flew in ...'

Shaun Bartlett scored Charlton Athletic's goal: 'O'Brien's knock fell in between Titus Bramble and Shaun Bartlett and it was the latter who reacted first to go in on goal and fire past Shay Given'.

19 The reporter suggests that Newcastle made a disappointing start to the season. Select and quote three phrases from paragraph 3 which tell you this. **(1 mark)**

Focus: Deduce, infer and interpret information and events or ideas from the text.

'Disappointing start to the campaign', 'hit bottom spot early on', 'depressing slump'.

20 What facts does the passage give about the Newcastle player whose family name is Robert? Copy and complete the fact-file. **(2 marks)**

Focus: Describe, select and retrieve information and events or ideas from the text. Use quotation and reference to the text.

Facts about Robert		The words which tell me this
Personal name	*Laurent*	*'Laurent Robert'*
Nationality	*French*	*'The Frenchman' (just after a sentence about Laurent Robert)*
Playing position	*Left wing*	*'The left-winger' (just after the words 'notably Laurent Robert')*
Transfer fee to Newcastle	*£10 million*	*'the £10m man's left-foot bullet' (following the words 'a low Robert drive')*

21 What does 'on the bench' mean in paragraph 10? **(2 marks)**

Focus: Comment on the writer's use of language, grammatical and literary features at word and sentence level.

'The bench' is the substitutes' bench. Readers can work this out from the following words: '... Michael Chopra named on the bench for the first time in his career. Chopra never entered the field of play...'.

22 To what extent does the report communicate the excitement of the match? **(4 marks)**

Focus: Identify and comment on the writer's purposes and viewpoints, and the effect of the text on the reader.

The beginning of the report has a slower pace than the part which describes the match itself, because it is mainly concerned with giving background information. Nonetheless, the pace is fairly brisk; this effect is created by the use of concise language such as '... the 69-year-old, still in pain after the match, was given a nice boost when he realised that rapidly rising Newcastle have the title contenders back in their sights'.

A great deal of information is communicated through the use of concise phrases ('still in pain after the match' and 'rapidly rising Newcastle').

The part of the report which describes the football match itself has a fast pace, which communicates an atmosphere of excitement. This is created partly by the use of concise expressions such as 'the front-man jinked his way past four players' and 'it was Charlton who took the lead'. An effect of excitement is communicated by the use of strong verbs, such as 'jinked', 'tipped over', 'robbed', 'powered' and 'flew in', and expressive adjectives such as 'superb', 'sweet', 'on-rushing' and 'neat'.

The long sentences, containing concise clauses and phrases, give a flowing effect: for example, 'But five minutes later the Irish goalkeeper could do nothing about the £10m man's left-foot bullet that flew in after some neat link-up play between Solano, Shearer and Ameobi'.

Test Paper 5 Mark scheme: Questions and assessment focuses

Question	Describe, select and retrieve information and events or ideas from the text. Use quotation and reference to the text.	Deduce, infer and interpret information and events or ideas from the text.	Comment on the structure and organisation of texts, grammatical and presentational features at text level.	Comment on the writer's use of language, grammatical and literary features at word and sentence level.	Identify and comment on the writer's purposes and viewpoints, and the effect of the text on the reader.
1:1	1				
1:2				2	
1:3				3 G	
1:4		2			
1:5	2				
1:6				2	
1:7					4
2:8			2		
2:9			2		
2:10				3	
2:11				2	
2:12		2			
2:13			3		
2:14					4
3:15	1				
3:16	1				
3:17	3				
3:18	2				
3:19		1			
3:20	2				
3:21				2	
3:22					4
Total	12	5	7	14	12

Focus and number of marks   (G: includes a focus on grammar)

Answers to Test Paper 6: News

Questions 1–8 are about *The Seeing Stone*

1   Find and copy three details from the passage which tell you that this book has a historical setting.   **(1 mark)**
    Focus: Describe, select and retrieve information and events or ideas from the text. Use quotation and reference to the text.
    Any three from: 'King Richard has been badly wounded', 'a French arrow', 'this manor', 'Prince John's not half the man his elder brother was', 'Far better King Richard's nephew became king', 'Prince Arthur', 'I fear for England if John is crowned king', 'Sir William's freeman', 'It was Norman or English'.

2   Why has the writer used ellipses in the following sentence? 'In the southwest of France, ma'am ... a castle on a hilltop ... Chalus ... I don't know, sir ... one of Count Aimar's ...'   **(2 marks)**
    Focus: Comment on the writer's use of language, grammatical and literary features at word and sentence level.
    The use of ellipses communicates a mixture of breathlessness and uncertainty on the part of the messenger, who is speaking. It suggests that he is answering several questions at once and has rushed to the house to give the family the message.

3   What does the messenger tell you in the broken sentence in question 2? Write three sentences to express it more clearly.   **(2 marks)**
    Focus: Deduce, infer and interpret information and events or ideas from the text.
    King Richard was in southwest France at a castle on a hilltop. The castle is at Chalus. The arrow which hit him was fired by one of Count Aimar's men.

4   Copy and complete the chart below to summarise what the passage tells you about the characters who appear in the passage.   **(2 marks)**
    Focus: Describe, select and retrieve information and events or ideas from the text. Use quotation and reference to the text.

Name, if known	Description (for example, approximate age) and other information	Relationship to the narrator, if known
one of Lord Stephen's riders	*male*	*not stated*
John	*a nobleman, Christian*	*father*
Nain (Welsh for 'grandmother')	*Welsh*	*grandmother*
not stated	*Christian*	*mother*
Serle	*male, enjoys poetry*	*not stated*
Thomas	*Sir William's freeman*	*not stated*

5   Which other kings had been injured by arrows before King Richard?   **(1 mark)**
    Focus: Describe, select and retrieve information and events or ideas from the text. Use quotation and reference to the text.
    'Harold' and 'Rufus'.

6   Explain in your own words what the narrator's father means when he says: 'We'll light candles. We'll get down on our knee-bones. Every man-jack living in this manor'. Why did he want to do this?   **(2 marks)**
    Focus: Deduce, infer and interpret information and events or ideas from the text.
    He means that he and everyone else in the manor will pray for the king (candles are often lit to accompany prayers and Christians often kneel for prayer).

7   Comment on the similarities and differences between the first and the second messages which are brought to the family, and the ways in which they are presented. **(2 marks)**

Focus: Deduce, infer and interpret information and events or ideas from the text.

The first message seems to have been brought in haste and the messenger does not appear to have thought a great deal about it (the way in which he answers, in a sentence broken by ellipses, suggests that he has difficulty in answering the questions he is asked). That message suggests that King Richard has been injured by an enemy arrow.

The second message, however, seems to be well thought out and much more detailed. We are not given the messenger's exact words, but the way in which his speech is reported makes it seem much more fluent and more careful than that of the first messenger. It is more precise, saying exactly where the king was ('King Richard had ridden up to the hilltop castle at Chalus with a dozen men, right up to the portcullis'). It says exactly where on his body the arrow hit him ('...pierced the top of the king's back. It came out through his neck...') and that it was from one of the king's own side and not an enemy ('...one of the king's own crossbowmen, supporting him from behind, fired short. ... No! Not a French arrow. It was Norman or English. It was loyal fire!').

8   How well does the writer communicate the contrasting reactions of the characters to the death of the king? **(4 marks)**

Focus: Identify and comment on the writer's purposes and viewpoints, and the effect of the text on the reader.

The tone of the passage is set as serious: 'We heard bad news today.' It develops an urgent atmosphere as the family question the messenger to find out the details about the king's injury: 'Then we all started asking questions at the same time ...'. This urgency is intensified by the messenger's broken speech: 'In the southwest of France, ma'am ... a castle on a hilltop ... Chalus ... I don't know, sir ... one of Count Aimar's ...'. The characters' reactions are communicated through dialogue. The narrator's father's words suggest that he accepts that God ordains people's fate, but that prayer can help ('Lord God gives life and Lord God takes it away', 'We'll light candles. We'll get down on our knee-bones ...'). He seems to be concerned with the political and financial implications of the king's death: 'If King Richard dies, it will be three times the worse for us ... a new king means a new tax ...'. He is concerned about what will happen if there is a new king (and who that king will be): 'Prince John's not half the man his elder brother was', 'Far better King Richard's nephew became king ... Prince Arthur'.

The narrator's mother seems to regret the king's death, despite the fact that she is Welsh and the English kings had been leading armies against the Welsh, because she values his personal achievements: 'He brought home a piece of the Holy Cross...', 'he roared and rattled the gates of the Saracens'.

The writer introduces humour in recounting the response of the narrator's grandmother, who mishears parts of the conversation: 'John says there'll be trouble.' 'Double?' 'No, mother. Trouble! Welsh trouble.'

Questions 9–16 are about *Unrelated Incidents 3*

9   The poem is written in the way in which it should be spoken. Rewrite in standard English the part which ends at the first full stop. **(2 marks)**

Focus: Comment on the structure and organisation of texts, grammatical and presentational features at text level.

'This is the six o'clock news,' the man said. 'And the reason I talk with a BBC accent is because you would not want me to talk about the truth with a voice like one of you scruff.'

10 Comment on the difference you made to the part of the poem which you rewrote in standard English. Explain why the poet wrote it as he did. **(2 marks)**

Focus: Comment on the structure and organisation of texts, grammatical and presentational features at text level.

The change to standard English makes the message sound much more insulting to the listeners. The writer might have used non-standard English to emphasise the cultural differences between people in positions of power or authority (such as those who decide what information to tell the public) and the general public themselves. It also suggests that the message is addressed to a particular section of the general public – those who do not speak standard English (and, by implication, people of low social classes, whom the newsreader addresses as 'you scruff').

Answers: Test Paper 6

11 What does the poet mean by a 'BBC accent'? **(1 mark)**
Focus: Deduce, infer and interpret information and events or ideas from the text.
He means standard English, spoken with little trace of a regional accent and no regional dialect words.

12 According to the poem, why do newsreaders have to read the news in a 'BBC accent'? **(2 marks)**
Focus: Comment on the writer's use of language, grammatical and literary features at word and sentence level.
If they speak in strong regional accents and use regional dialect and not standard English, no one will take them seriously: 'if / a toktaboot / thi trooth / lik wana yoo / scruff yi / widny thingk / it wuz troo.'

13 According to the poem, why do the people to whom the newsreader is speaking not know the truth? **(2 marks)**
Focus: Identify and comment on the writer's purposes and viewpoints, and the effect of the text on the reader.
They do not know the truth because they do not speak correctly:
'yooz doant no / thi trooth / yirsellz cawz / yi canny talk / right.'

14 Select and copy a sentence, clause or phrase which suggests that the newsreader does not respect the listeners, and explain how it does so. **(2 marks)**
Focus: Deduce, infer and interpret information and events or ideas from the text.
He tells them, in effect, to shut up and listen to him ('this is / the six a clock / nyooz. belt up.') because, since they cannot speak properly, they cannot know the truth.

15 What is the message of the poem? **(3 marks)**
Focus: Deduce, infer and interpret information and events or ideas from the text.
Either of the following, or any response which is supported by references to the poem:
The message given by the poem seems to be the following: if people speak in standard English they are more likely to be taken seriously than people who do not. At first it seems to be addressing on their own terms those who do not speak standard English – explaining why they are not listened to – but it develops a sneering tone when it tells the listeners 'If I talk about the truth like one of you scruff, you would not think it was true. Just one of you scruff talking', 'You don't know the truth because you cannot talk right'.
The poem could, however, be taken as a coded message to 'the masses' who do not speak standard English and are regarded by some people as 'scruff': it is in a language which they can understand but which might not be understood by people who speak standard English. It could be saying: 'If you want to be heard, change your way of speaking and smarten yourselves up'.

16 How successful is the poem in expressing views about social class, as shown by the way in which people speak? **(4 marks)**
Focus: Identify and comment on the writer's purposes and viewpoints, and the effect of the text on the reader.
The poem suggests that social class is expressed by accent ('if / a toktaboot / thi trooth / lik wanna yoo / scruff'). This quotation links accent and dress ('yoo scruff'). The poet could be expressing the view that people who do not speak standard English cannot be taken seriously; or he could be saying that people make superficial judgements about others who do not speak standard English (suggesting that they cannot possibly know anything if they do not 'speak properly').
These views are expressed through the use of the form of a television news broadcast presented in non-standard English; but the news is an expression of views about the links between the ways in which people speak and their knowledge (and therefore power and influence – you need to speak properly to be taken seriously).
The poem is in the form of a rap; this is not the rhythm of a television or radio news broadcast. The rap gives the poem an informal feel, as does the use of non-standard English. This provides a contrast with a real news programme; it also gives it humour, as does the use of expressions such as 'wanna yoo scruff'.

Questions 17–23 are about *Chicken fat to power lorries*

17 Find and copy three pieces of information which suggest why chicken fat is a better fuel than conventional diesel oil. **(2 marks)**
Focus: Describe, select and retrieve information and events or ideas from the text. Use quotation and reference to the text.
Any three examples from the following:
It attracts a lower taxation rate: 'biodiesel refiners ... given a 20p-a-litre green tax concession ...'

It is cheaper: 'A much cheaper alternative to diesel', 'The 32p-a-litre fuel supply – compared with 73p at forecourt diesel pumps', 'will ... undercut conventional diesel prices by at least 10p a litre', 'Converting an in-house product like the waste oil will add to savings for the firm'.

It is better for the environment: 'chip pan fuel emissions are up to 40% lower than diesel', 'Oil's a finite resource ... we shouldn't be wasting it'.

18 What do you think 'biodiesel' means?   **(1 mark)**
    Focus: Deduce, infer and interpret information and events or ideas from the text.
    'Bio' comes from 'biological', which means 'concerning living things'. Its root is 'bio' (Greek, 'life'). 'Diesel' is a fuel oil for diesel engines. The combination of 'diesel' with the prefix 'bio' suggests a diesel fuel oil which is made from living material, rather than from petrochemicals.

19 Find and copy two phrases in paragraph 4 which have opposite meanings. Explain their meanings.   **(2 marks)**
    Focus: Describe, select and retrieve information and events or ideas from the text. Use quotation and reference to the text
    Two phrases which have opposite meanings in paragraph 4 are 'disposal headache' and 'potential money-earner'. Asda had problems in disposing of the used cooking oil from its canteens – and disposal costs the company money (hence 'disposal headache'). Instead of having to find a way of disposing of the oil, the company can use it to make a profit ('potential money-earner').

20 Explain the play on words in 'frying squad'. Describe the picture it creates in your mind.   **(2 marks)**
    Focus: Comment on the writer's use of language, grammatical and literary features at word and sentence level.
    Any answer is acceptable which builds on the explanation of the pun. The following is an example: The play on words links the idea of the police 'flying squad' and the oil used for frying food. It suggests a picture of police officers flying through the air or dashing along the roads in vehicles shaped like chip pans.

21 Find and copy as many words or phrases as you can which are used as nouns for the new fuel.   **(2 marks)**
    Focus: Describe, select and retrieve information and events or ideas from the text. Use quotation and reference to the text.
    'biodiesel', 'chip pan fuel', 'extra-value cooking oil'.

22 Explain why the reporter uses so many different words and phrases for the same fuel.   **(2 marks)**
    Focus: Deduce, infer and interpret information and events or ideas from the text.
    The reporter refers to the ingredients of the fuel in the names he gives it; this helps readers to understand what it is made from. It also creates humour ('chip pan fuel' conjures up a humorous picture of people pouring the contents of their chip pans into the fuel tanks of trucks).

23 How successful has the writer been in attracting the attention of readers and keeping their attention throughout the report?   **(5 marks)**
    Focus: Identify and comment on the writer's purposes and viewpoints, and the effect of the text on the reader.
    Any response is acceptable which is supported by reference to the text. The following are examples:
    The headline sounds incredible; readers expect this to be an 'April Fool'. They probably check the date of the newspaper. This humorous headline attracts readers' attention, and their attention is maintained by the humorous tone of the report itself: for example, the play on the words 'frying squad' and the description of police officers sniffing out the illegal use of the fuel: '... tactics included sniffing out the chip-shop smell of bootleg cars'.
    The introduction sets the scene by giving some background information about how Asda discovered that the cooking oil it was paying people to take away was being used in a 'scam' as a fuel. The details of the 'scam' are not given until the end of the report; this keeps readers interested – they want to know the details.
    The manufacture of the fuel is made clear without actually giving the readers a recipe for making it illegally; they are informed that it is made from waste cooking oil with methanol added.
    The report has a lively and fast pace which is achieved through the use of concise language which makes use of noun phrases, such as 'company trials', 'chip pan fuel', 'innocent involvement', 'moonshine operation', 'disposal headache' and 'potential money-earner'.

Test Paper 6 Mark scheme: Questions and assessment focuses

Question	Describe, select and retrieve information and events or ideas from the text. Use quotation and reference to the text.	Deduce, infer and interpret information and events or ideas from the text.	Comment on the structure and organisation of texts, grammatical and presentational features at text level.	Comment on the writer's use of language, grammatical and literary features at word and sentence level.	Identify and comment on the writer's purposes and viewpoints, and the effect of the text on the reader.
	Focus and number of marks (G: includes a focus on grammar)				
1:1	1				
1:2				2 G	
1:3		2 G			
1:4	2				
1:5	1				
1:6		2			
1:7		2			
1:8					4
2:9			2 G		
2:10			2 G		
2:11		1			
2:12				2	
2:13					2
2:14		2			
2:15		3			
2:16					4
3:17	2				
3:18		1			
3:19	2				
3:20				2	
3:21	2				
3:22		2			
3:23					5
Total	10	15	4	6	15

Testing KS3 English Year 7 © Nelson Thornes 2003

Storms

The theme linking these three reading texts is 'Storms'.
- You have 1 hour and 15 minutes to answer the questions on the three passages.
- You are given 15 minutes' reading time before this.

Reading test 1

Reading and interpreting a passage from *The Great Storm of 1987* adapted from the Met Office website

The Great Storm of 1987

In southern England, 15 million trees were lost, among them many valuable specimens. Trees blocked roads and railways and brought down electricity and telephone lines. Hundreds of thousands of homes in England remained without power for more than 24 hours.

Falling trees and masonry damaged or destroyed buildings and cars. Numerous small boats were wrecked or blown away. A ship capsized at Dover, and a Channel ferry was driven ashore near Folkestone.

The storm killed 18 people in England and at least four more in France. The death toll might have been far greater had the storm struck in the daytime.

The storm gathers

Four or five days before the storm struck, forecasters predicted severe weather on the following Thursday or Friday. By mid-week, however, guidance from weather prediction models was somewhat equivocal. Instead of stormy weather over a considerable part of the UK, the models suggested that severe weather would reach no farther north than the English Channel and coastal parts of southern England.

During the afternoon of 15 October, winds were very light over most parts of the UK. The pressure gradient was slack. A depression was drifting slowly northwards over the North Sea off eastern Scotland. A col lay over England, Wales and Ireland. Over the Bay of Biscay, a depression was developing.

It's clear that for sea areas, warnings of severe weather were both timely and adequate. Forecasts for land areas, however, left much to be desired.

During the evening of 15 October, radio and TV forecasts mentioned strong winds but indicated that heavy rain would be the main feature, rather than strong winds. By the time most people went to bed, exceptionally strong winds hadn't been mentioned in national radio and TV weather broadcasts.

Warnings of severe weather had been issued, however, to various agencies and emergency authorities, including the London Fire Brigade. Perhaps the most important warning was issued by the Met Office to the Ministry of Defence at 0135 UTC, 16 October. It warned that the expected consequences of the storm were such that civil authorities might need to call on assistance from the military.

In south-east England, where the greatest damage occurred, gusts of 70 knots or more were recorded continually for three or four consecutive hours.

A hurricane or not

TV weather presenter Michael Fish will long be remembered for telling viewers, the evening before the storm struck, that there would be no hurricane. But he was unfortunate. Fish was referring to a tropical cyclone over the western part of the North Atlantic Ocean that day. This storm, he said, would not reach the British Isles – and it didn't.

It's worthwhile to consider whether or not the storm was, in any sense, a hurricane – the description applied to it by so many people.

In the Beaufort scale of wind force, Hurricane Force (Force 12) is defined as a wind of 64 knots or more, sustained over a period of at least 10 minutes. Gusts, which are comparatively short-lived (but cause much of the destruction), are not taken into account. By this definition, Hurricane Force winds occurred locally but were not widespread.

A 10-minute mean wind speed of 70 knots (an average over 10 minutes) was recorded at Lee on Solent in Hampshire, and an hourly-mean speed of 68 knots at Gorleston. The highest hourly-mean speed recorded in the UK was 75 knots, at the Royal Sovereign Lighthouse. Winds reached Force 11 (56-63 knots) in many coastal regions of south-east England. Inland, however, their strength was considerably less. At the London Weather Centre, for example, the mean wind speed did not exceed 44 knots (Force 9). At Gatwick Airport, it never exceeded 34 knots (Force 8).

The Great Storm of 1987 did not originate in the Tropics and was not, by any definition, a hurricane – but it was certainly exceptional.

Once every 200 years

South-east of a line extending from Southampton through north London to Great Yarmouth, gust speeds and mean wind speeds were as great as those which can be expected to recur, on average, no more frequently than once in 200 years; so comparison with the great storm of 1703 was justified. The storm of 1987 was remarkable for its ferocity, and affected much the same area of the UK as its 1703 counterpart.

Questions 1–7 are about *The Great Storm of 1987*

1   Find and copy three effects of the storm. **(2 marks)**
    Focus: Describe, select and retrieve information and events or ideas from the text. Use quotation and reference to the text.

_____

_____

_____

_____

_____

2 Explain why 'The death toll might have been far greater had the storm struck in the daytime'.

(2 marks)

Focus: Deduce, infer and interpret information and events or ideas from the text.

_____

_____

_____

_____

_____

_____

3 Say what you think 'equivocal', used earlier in the sentence, might mean from reading the sentence below. (2 marks)

Focus: Deduce, infer and interpret information and events or ideas from the text.

> Instead of stormy weather over a considerable part of the UK, the models suggested that severe weather would reach no farther north than the English Channel and coastal parts of southern England.

_____

_____

_____

_____

_____

_____

4 Select and quote three examples of technical language about the subject which show that this comes from the website of an official organisation. (2 marks)

Focus: Describe, select and retrieve information and events or ideas from the text. Use quotation and reference to the text.

_____

_____

_____

_____

_____

_____

_____

_____

5 Comment on the reasons for the different uses of dashes and hyphens in the following examples. **(2 marks)**

Focus: Comment on the writer's use of language, grammatical and literary features at word and sentence level.

This storm, he said, would not reach the British Isles – and it didn't.	South-east of a line extending from Southampton …
The Great Storm of 1987 did not originate in the Tropics and was not, by any definition, a hurricane – but it was certainly exceptional.	A 10-minute mean wind speed of 70 knots …

_____

_____

_____

_____

_____

_____

_____

_____

_____

6 Write the events of the passage in a time chart. **(2 marks)**

Focus: Comment on the structure and organisation of texts, grammatical and presentational features at text level.

Four or five days before	
Afternoon of 15 October	
Evening of 15 October	
16 October	

_____

_____

_____

_____

_____

_____

Testing KS3 English Year 7 © Nelson Thornes 2003

7   The writer has to explain that the storm was very serious but that it was not a 'hurricane' in the scientific sense. How successful is he?

You should write about:
- the use of information to support the statements made
- the use of precise, technical detail
- the structure and organisation of the facts
- the way in which he comments on what Michael Fish said.   **(4 marks)**

Focus: Comment on the writer's use of language, grammatical and literary features at word and sentence level.

_____

_____

_____

_____

_____

_____

_____

_____

_____

_____

_____

_____

_____

_____

_____

Reading test 2

Reading and interpreting a poem by Ted Hughes

Wind

This house has been far out at sea all night,
The woods crashing through darkness, the booming hills,
Wind stampeding the fields under the windows
Floundering black astride and blinding wet

Till day rose. Then, under an orange sky,
The hills had new places, and wind wielded
Blade-light, luminous black and emerald
Flexing like the lens of a mad eye.

At noon I scaled along the house-side as far as
The coal-house door. I dared once to look up:
Through the brunt wind that dented the balls of my eyes
The tent of the hills drummed and strained its guy-rope,

The fields quivering, the skyline a grimace,
At any second to bang and vanish with a flap:
The wind flung a magpie away, and a black
Back gull bent like an iron bar slowly. The house

Rang like some fine green goblet in the note
That any second would shatter it. Now deep
In chairs, in front of the great fire, we grip
Our hearts and cannot entertain book, thought,

Or each other. We watch the fire blazing,
And feel the roots of the house move, but sit on,
Seeing the window tremble to come in,
Hearing the stones cry out under the horizons.

Questions 8–14 are about *Wind*

8   Quote two examples of personification from the first verse.   **(2 marks)**
    Focus: Describe, select and retrieve information and events or ideas from the text. Use quotation and reference to the text.

_____

_____

_____

_____

9   State which verbs are used to describe the actions of both. Explain how these show the effect of
    the storm.   **(2 marks)**
    Focus: Deduce, infer and interpret information and events or ideas from the text.

    _____

    _____

    _____

    _____

    _____

    _____

    _____

    _____

10 What impression does the onomatopoeic adjective 'booming' (line 2) give of the effect of the
    storm on the countryside?   **(1 mark)**
    Focus: Comment on the writer's use of language, grammatical and literary features at word and sentence level.

    _____

    _____

    _____

    _____

    _____

    _____

    _____

11 Look carefully at the structure of the poem. Using the chart write in the numbers of the verses
    which deal with the world _outside_ and the world _inside_.   **(2 marks)**
    Focus: Comment on the structure and organisation of texts, grammatical and presentational features at text level.

Verses describing outside	Verses describing inside
1,	

    _____

    _____

    _____

    _____

12 'The wind flung a magpie away, and a black / Back gull bent like an iron bar slowly.'
   a. What does the metaphor 'flung' tell the reader about the storm?
   b. Explain how the simile 'bent like an iron bar' creates an effective image of a bird flying in the face of a storm. **(2 marks)**
   Focus: Comment on the writer's use of language, grammatical and literary features at word and sentence level.

_____

_____

_____

_____

_____

_____

13 In the last two verses of the poem, the writer considers the effects of the storm on people in the house. Find words the poet uses to give an impression of their state of mind: for example, why are they 'deep in their chairs'? Why do they 'grip their hearts'?
   Look at what they are doing, what this means and the way this is described. **(2 marks)**
   Focus: Comment on the writer's use of language, grammatical and literary features at word and sentence level.

_____

_____

_____

_____

_____

_____

14 Ted Hughes is known as a very 'physical' poet: readers can feel through their senses what it would have been like to experience the storm. How successfully do you think he has created this effect in 'Wind'?
   You could write about:
   ● the way he communicates the strength and violence of the wind through his images
   ● the way he shows how people react to it
   ● any other examples of the senses being appealed to. **(5 marks)**
   Focus: Identify and comment on the writer's purposes and viewpoints, and the effect of the text on the reader.

_____

_____

_____

_____

_____

_____

Reading test 3

Reading and interpreting a passage from *The Night the Water Came* by Clive King

In this extract, Apu describes a cyclone which struck his island in the Indian Ocean and how he survived.

My favourite climbing tree is the big branchy one with the thick trunk that stands near our house. (I mean, it used to stand there. I still can't get used to the idea that it's gone.)

When Uncle woke me it was very dark and I could hear the wind blowing hard and roaring in the branches of the tree. He hurried me outside and I couldn't even see the stars, so the sky must have been covered with clouds. It seemed an odd time to be climbing trees and I started to ask questions, but Uncle told me not to argue and to get climbing.

I knew the best way up with my eyes shut. I felt for the low branch above my head, pulled myself up until I could hook my leg over it and hoisted myself up and on to it. I called to Uncle that I was up, and he shouted, 'Higher! Higher!' I felt for the branches and stumps that I knew and climbed upwards until I was clinging to a thin branch that was tossing and swaying and seemed to be doing its best to throw me off.

The grownups were arguing in the darkness below. My uncle was trying to persuade my aunts and cousins to climb up too. I really thought he'd gone crazy like the man in the village on the other side of the island who sometimes sits in the trees like a monkey. (I mean he used to, he's not there any more.) Uncle kept shouting, 'The water's coming! The water's coming!' Of course he was right, it did come. I don't know how he knew.

Above the noise of the wind in the branches I could hear some of the words of the argument going on below me. Uncle was shouting, 'Up the tree!' Other voices were saying, 'Not that one', or 'To the boats! To the boats!' I shouted down, 'Come on. I'll help you!' But of course none of them could climb as well as me: they were either too old or too young. I don't think any of them got into my tree.

The wind tore at me and the branches thrashed about me but I was beginning to see things better. It was still nearly pitch dark but suddenly there was something darker and blacker flying through the air like a huge bat and wrapping itself round the lower branches of my tree. I heard the women's voices wailing, 'The roof! The roof!', and I knew it was the thatch of our house going to pieces. I'd seen this happen before. Roofs blow off quite often in the islands, and quite often the water comes up nearly to the top of the mound on which our house is built. But we'd never climbed trees in the middle of the night before.

When the water came it was different from other times. I could hear a roaring of water approaching even above the noise of the wind in the trees and then suddenly it was rushing around the trunk of the tree and pouring over the lower branches. I mean, it didn't rise slowly like the other floods I'd seen; it was halfway up the trunk all at once and I was wet with spray in the highest branches. And then the whole tree seemed to be moving. Yes, I know the branches had been moving but now I had the feeling that everything was slowly toppling, and then I was in the water though I was still holding the branch. And now it was the water instead of the wind that was trying to tear me off the branch, and the rough bark was hurting the skin on my chest and arms as I clung for my life. I struggled and reached for branches above me, caught one and pulled myself clear of the water. There were great salt waves washing over the tree. I could taste them and my eyes stung as I tried to climb above them. The tree was lying right over on its side, and climbing it was quite different. I reached a branch that was clear of the waves and clung on with my arms and legs.

The water didn't seem to be rushing round the trunk as it had been and in the darkness the tops of the other trees seemed to be moving away. Then I knew I was afloat, and alone in the darkness and the storm.

How should I know how long I floated, or how far? All I knew was that I must hang on. Though the current didn't drag at the tree, now that we were floating along with it, the wind still tugged at me and the spray broke over me. The night seemed without end. I even thought that perhaps the sun had been washed away too and it would never return.

Questions 15–22 are about *The Night the Water Came*

15 Find and copy two signs which showed Apu that the storm was approaching.   **(2 marks)**
  Focus: Describe, select and retrieve information and events or ideas from the text. Use quotation and reference to the text.

_____

_____

_____

_____

_____

_____

16 Explain why the writer uses brackets in the following two examples.   **(2 marks)**
  Focus: Comment on the writer's use of language, grammatical and literary features at word and sentence level.

> (I mean, it used to stand there. I still can't get used to the idea that it's gone.)
> (I mean he used to, he's not there any more.)

_____

_____

_____

_____

_____

_____

17 Why did it seem like 'an odd time to be climbing trees'? **(2 marks)**
   Focus: Describe, select and retrieve information and events or ideas from the text. Use quotation and reference to the text.

_____

_____

_____

_____

_____

_____

_____

_____

_____

_____

_____

_____

18 Describe and explain the reasons for the different reactions of the adults and Apu as the storm approached. **(2 marks)**
   Focus: Deduce, infer and interpret information and events or ideas from the text.

_____

_____

_____

_____

_____

_____

_____

_____

_____

_____

_____

19

> … but suddenly there was something darker and blacker flying through the air like a huge bat and wrapping itself round the lower branches of my tree.

What was Apu describing? Show how the writer's use of the simile helps us to imagine the scene better. **(2 marks)**
Focus: Comment on the writer's use of language, grammatical and literary features at word and sentence level.

_____

_____

_____

_____

_____

_____

_____

_____

_____

20 List two verbs used to describe the impact of the water and explain how they add to the impression of the storm. **(2 marks)**
Focus: Comment on the writer's use of language, grammatical and literary features at word and sentence level.

_____

_____

_____

_____

_____

_____

_____

_____

_____

_____

21 How do we know that the tree containing Apu fell into the water from the sea?　　**(1 mark)**
   Focus: Deduce, infer and interpret information and events or ideas from the text.

_____

_____

_____

_____

_____

_____

_____

_____

_____

_____

_____

22 Apu writes in a first-person narrative. How important is this to the author's intention of showing us the ferocity of the storm and what it would have been like to be at the centre of it?
   You should write about:
   ● how we get a sense of the oncoming storm through the narrator
   ● how we get a sense of the reactions of other characters to the storm
   ● what it was like at the centre of the storm clinging to the tree
   ● the feelings Apu experiences at various parts of the narrative.　　**(5 marks)**
   Focus: Identify and comment on the writer's purposes and viewpoints, and the effect of the text on the reader.

_____

_____

_____

_____

_____

_____

_____

_____

_____

_____

Storms

These two writing assignments are linked to the theme of 'Storms'.

Major task

- You should spend about 40 minutes on this.
- There are 30 marks available.

Write a description of what you imagine it was like to be out on the night of the Great Storm of 1987.

Think about these points:
- Use information from the passage about the weather conditions.
- Choose information from the other two passages to use in your description.
- Why are you out?
- How does the storm develop?
- What are you thinking and feeling at various stages?

Planning notes:
- Before you start writing, use the format on this page to help you to plan and write notes.
- Allow time to read your work and check your use of language before you finish.

Introduction Why you were outdoors at night	**The storm begins** Signs? What happens in the environment around you? How do you feel? What do you do?
You realise that this is a serious storm What is it like? What do you do? What do you think and feel?	**The height of the storm** Describe what happens around you
The storm lessens How do you know? How do you feel?	**Conclusion**

Minor task

- You should spend about 25 minutes on this.
- There are 20 marks available.

Imagine that you have been told that there will be a serious storm and that you will have to spend the night at school because you cannot get home.
Write an information sheet for other pupils giving them some indication of what will happen in school and how they need to behave in case of emergency.

You should write only three paragraphs to:
- inform the reader of your views
- advise them so that they will do as you say.

Do not use the same information as you included in your answer to the major writing task.

Planning notes:
- Before you start writing, use the format on this page to help you to plan and write notes.
- Organise your ideas into three paragraphs only.
- Allow time to read your work and check your use of language before you finish.

Explain the situation	What will the sleeping arrangements be?
What are the rules 'in case of emergency'?	What will you eat and where will the food come from?
Will you have any advice in case of floods?	What about first aid?

The way we treat animals

The theme linking these three reading texts is 'The way we treat animals'.
- You have 1 hour and 15 minutes to answer the questions on the three passages.
- You are given 15 minutes' reading time before this.

Reading test 1

Reading and interpreting a passage from *The Rats of NIMH* by Robert C O'Brien

In a minute or so I felt myself being lifted up; and swinging back and forth in the net, I was carried with my three companions to the white truck I had seen earlier. Its back doors were open, and it was lighted inside. I could see that its whole interior was a large wire cage. Into this our net was thrust; the man then opened the draw string and we were dumped on to the floor, which was covered with sawdust. The other nets were emptied one at a time the same way; and in a few minutes there was a good-sized crowd of us on the floor, all more or less dazed and all (if I was typical) terrified. The cage was locked, the doors clanged shut, and the lights went out. I heard the truck motor start; a second later the floor lurched beneath me. We were moving. Where were they taking us? For what purpose?

'Nicodemus?' It was Jenner. You can imagine how glad I was to hear him. But I was sorry, too.

'Jenner. I thought maybe you got away.'

'I was in the last net. I thought I saw you across the floor.'

'Where are we going?'

'I don't know.'

'What's a lab?'

'A laboratory.'

'Yes, but what is it?'

'I don't know. I've just heard the word somewhere.'

'Well, I think that's where we're going. Whatever it is.'

The truck rumbled along through the dark, over bumpy streets at first, then, at a higher speed, over a smooth road. There were no windows in the back, so it was impossible to see where we were going – not that I would have known anyway, never before having been more than half a dozen streets from home. I think we drove for about two hours, but it might have been less, before the truck slowed down, and turned, and finally came to a stop.

The back doors were opened again, and through the wire wall of the cage I saw that we had come to a building, very modern, of white cement and glass. It was square and big, about ten storeys tall. Night had fallen, and most of its windows were dark, but the platform to which our truck drove us was lighted, and there were people waiting for us.

A door opened, and three men came out. One of them pushed a cart, a trolley piled with small wire cages. The man beside him was dressed in a heavy coat, boots and thick leather gloves. The third man wore heavy horn-rimmed glasses and a white coat. He was obviously the leader.

The men from the truck, the ones who had caught us, now joined the men from the building.

'How many did you get?' asked the man in the white coat.

'Hard to count – they keep moving around. But I make it between sixty and seventy.'

'Good. Any trouble?'

'No. It was easy. They acted almost tame.'

'I hope not. I've got enough tame ones.'

'Oh, they're lively enough. And they look healthy.'

'Let's get them out.'

The man with the gloves and the boots then donned a wire face-mask as well, and climbed in among us. He opened a small sliding trapdoor at the back of our cage; a man outside held one of the small cages up to the opening, and one at a time we were pushed out into our individual little prisons. A few of the rats snarled and tried to bite; I did not, and neither did Jenner; it was too obviously futile. When it was finished, the man in the white coat said, 'Sixty-three – good work.' A man from the trolley said, 'Thanks, Dr Schultz.' And we were stacked on the hand truck and wheeled into the building.

Dr Schultz. I did not know it then, but I was to be his prisoner (and his pupil) for the next three years.

We spent the rest of that night in a long white room. It was, in fact, a laboratory, with a lot of equipment at one end that I didn't understand at all then – bottles and shiny metal things and black boxes with wires trailing from them. But our end held only rows of cages or shelves, each cage with a tag on it, and each separated from its neighbours by wooden partitions on both sides. Someone came around with a stack of small jars and fastened one to my cage; a little pipe led through the bars like a sipping straw – drinking water. Then the lights were dimmed and we were left alone.

That cage was my home for a long time. It was not uncomfortable; it had a floor of some kind of plastic; medium soft and warm to the touch; with wire walls and ceiling, it was airy enough. Yet just the fact that it was a cage made it horrible. I, who had always run where I wanted, could go three hops forward, three hops back again, and that was all. But worse was the dreadful feeling – I know we all had it – that we were completely at the mercy of someone we knew not at all, for some purpose we could not guess. What were their plans for us?

As it turned out, the uncertainty itself was the worst suffering we had to undergo. We were treated well enough, except for some very small, very quick flashes of pain, which were part of our training. And we were always well fed, though the food, scientifically compiled pellets, was not what you'd call delicious.

But of course we didn't know that when we arrived, and I doubt that any of us got much sleep that first night. I know I didn't. So, in a way, it was a relief when early the next morning the lights snapped on and Dr Schultz entered. There were two other people with him, a young man and a young woman. Like him, they were dressed in white laboratory coats. He was talking to them as they entered the room and walked towards our cages.

'...three groups. Twenty for training on injection series A, twenty on series B. That will leave twenty-three for the control group. They get no injections at all – except, to keep the test exactly even, we will prick them with a plain needle. Let's call the groups A, B, and C for control; tag them and number them A-1 to A-20, B-1 to B-20, and so on. Number the cages the same way, and keep each rat in the same cage throughout. Diet will be the same for all.'

'When do we start the injections?'

'As soon as we're through with the tagging. We'll do that now. George, you number the tags and the cages. Julie, you tie them on. I'll hold.'

Test Paper 8: Reading

Questions 1–8 are about *The Rats of NIMH*

1 Quote the verb used in the first sentence which gives us the impression of what the movement
   was like when being carried in a net.   **(1 mark)**
   **Focus: Describe, select and retrieve information and events or ideas from the text. Use quotation and reference
   to the text.**

   _____

   _____

   _____

   _____

   _____

2 Find and copy two things which the narrator noticed about the inside of the van.   **(2 marks)**
   **Focus: Describe, select and retrieve information and events or ideas from the text. Use quotation and reference
   to the text.**

   _____

   _____

   _____

   _____

   _____

   _____

   _____

   _____

3 Explain in your own words how the rats felt about being captured in this way.   **(1 mark)**
   Focus: Deduce, infer and interpret information and events or ideas from the text.

   _____

   _____

   _____

   _____

   _____

   _____

   _____

4   Look at the passages of speech. How does the reader know which of the characters is
     speaking?   **(2 marks)**
     Focus: Comment on the writer's use of language, grammatical and literary features at word and sentence level.

    _____

    _____

    _____

    _____

    _____

    _____

    _____

5   Explain why 'You can imagine how glad I was to hear him. But I was sorry, too'.   **(2 marks)**
     Focus: Deduce, infer and interpret information and events or ideas from the text.

    _____

    _____

    _____

    _____

    _____

    _____

    _____

6   List the details you are given about the building to which the rats were taken. What feelings
     does this description evoke in the reader?   **(3 marks)**
     **Focus: Describe, select and retrieve information and events or ideas from the text. Use quotation and reference
     to the text.**

    _____

    _____

    _____

    _____

    _____

    _____

    _____

    _____

7 Quote two examples to show that this is a first-person narrative. How does using a first-person narrative make us feel more sympathetic towards the character? **(2 marks)**
   Focus: Comment on the writer's use of language, grammatical and literary features at word and sentence level.

_____

_____

_____

_____

_____

_____

_____

_____

_____

8 'That cage was my home for a long time.' Explain the rat's attitude towards the cage and how the author's description makes the reader feel.
   You should write about:
   ● the good aspects of the cage
   ● the bad aspects of the rat's life in the cage
   ● the examples the author uses to prove his point
   ● what you think the author feels about it
   ● what you feel about it. **(4 marks)**
   Focus: Identify and comment on the writer's purposes and viewpoints, and the effect of the text on the reader.

_____

_____

_____

_____

_____

_____

_____

_____

_____

_____

Reading test 2
Reading and interpreting a poem by James Kirkup

The Caged Bird in Springtime

What can it be,
This curious anxiety?
It is as if I wanted
To fly away from here.

But how absurd!
I have never flown in my life,
And I do not know
What flying means, though I have heard,
Of course, something about it.

Why do I peck the wires of this little cage?
It is the only nest I have ever known.
But I want to build my own,
High in the secret branches of the air.

I cannot quite remember how
It is done, but I know
That what I want to do
Cannot be done here.

I have all I need – seed and water, air and light.
Why, then, do I weep with anguish,
And beat my head with my wings
Against these sharp wires, while the children
Smile at each other, saying: 'Hark how he sings'?

Questions 9–16 are about *The Caged Bird in Springtime*

9 In verse 1, the bird is curious about a new feeling. What is it? **(1 mark)**
Focus: Describe, select and retrieve information and events or ideas from the text. Use quotation and reference to the text.

_____

_____

_____

_____

10 What evidence can you find to show that this is a first-person narration?   **(1 mark)**
   Focus: Comment on the structure and organisation of texts, grammatical and presentational features at text level.

_____

_____

_____

_____

_____

_____

_____

11 Say what you think is the subject of each verse, and how the poet introduces this in the first
   line of each verse.   **(4 marks)**
   Focus: Comment on the structure and organisation of texts, grammatical and presentational features at text level.

Verse	Subject	First line quotation
1		
2		
3		
4		
5		

_____

_____

_____

12 Explain the effect on the reader of the use of the adjectives in the following descriptions:
   'this _little_ cage ...', 'these _sharp_ wires...'.   **(3 marks)**
   Focus: Comment on the writer's use of language, grammatical and literary features at word and sentence level.

_____

_____

_____

_____

_____

_____

13 Explain the metaphor 'the secret branches of the air' and its effect.   **(2 marks)**
   Focus: Comment on the writer's use of language, grammatical and literary features at word and sentence level.

_____

_____

_____

_____

_____

_____

_____

_____

_____

_____

_____

_____

14 When the bird says, 'I have all I need', explain why this is not the case.   **(2 marks)**
   Focus: Deduce, infer and interpret information and events or ideas from the text.

_____

_____

_____

_____

_____

_____

_____

_____

_____

_____

_____

_____

15

> ... Against these sharp wires, while the children
> Smile at each other, saying: 'Hark how he sings'?

Explain the real reason for the bird's singing and how the children's misconception about the bird makes you feel. **(2 marks)**

Focus: Deduce, infer and interpret information and events or ideas from the text.

_____

_____

_____

_____

_____

_____

_____

_____

_____

_____

16 How do you feel about the bird in the cage?
You should write about:
- the meaning of the title
- the actions of the bird
- what it feels
- the way the writer describes feelings. **(4 marks)**

Focus: Identify and comment on the writer's purposes and viewpoints, and the effect of the text on the reader.

_____

_____

_____

_____

_____

_____

_____

_____

_____

Reading test 3
Reading and interpreting a non-fiction text

UK Zoos: Fit for life?

In the UK, an estimated ¼ million animals – large and small – are held in more than 400 zoological collections*.

Since 1984, these zoos have been regulated by the UK Zoo Licensing Act 1981 which aims to promote minimum standards of welfare, meaningful education, effective conservation, valuable research and essential public safety.

In the last 20 years, UK zoos have had to contend with growing levels of public scepticism and concern as more and more people question their justification.

Now they face a major new challenge. The recent introduction of the European Zoos Directive (1999/22/EC) by the European Union places an even greater emphasis on conservation, education, research and welfare.

Can UK zoos meet this new challenge and reassure an increasingly concerned public? This Official Zoo Health Check 2000 is the first of a series of independent and comprehensive zoo investigations by a team of scientists from the renowned international wildlife charity, the Born Free Foundation.

Recording key data over a 12-month period in more than 100 UK zoological collections, the Official Zoo Health Check 2000 seeks to assess for the first time the true 'health' of the UK zoo industry. Based on extensive research undertaken throughout 2000, this is the first of a series of reports to be published on the 'health' of UK zoos.

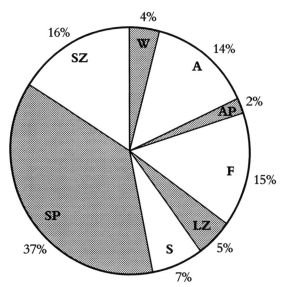

A= Aquaria
AP= Amusement Parks
F= Farm with exotics
LZ= Large Zoo
S= Sanctuary
SP= Specialised Collection
SZ= Small Zoo
W= Wildlife/Safari Park

*UK zoological collections – any collection of captive animals on a particular site, of which one individual or more belongs to a species not normally domesticated in the UK, open to the public seven or more days in 12 consecutive months (UK Zoo Licensing Act 1981).

Fig 1. Proportions of UK zoological collection types

Methodology
The Official Zoo Health Check 2000 scientifically investigated 104 randomly selected zoological collections representing 25% of all UK zoos: 'large' and 'small' zoos; safari parks; aquaria; amusement parks with exotic animals; open farms with exotic animals; sanctuaries with exotics open to the public; and specialised zoological collections (see fig. 1). All these collections comply with the definition of a zoo as set out in the current UK Zoo Licensing Act 1981. The findings therefore accurately represent the general state of all UK zoos.

Questions 17–22 are about *UK Zoos: Fit for Life?*

17

> In the UK, an estimated $\frac{1}{4}$ million animals – large and small – are held in more than 400 zoological collections*.

Explain the purpose of the asterisk. **(1 mark)**
Focus: Comment on the writer's use of language, grammatical and literary features at word and sentence level.

_____

_____

_____

_____

_____

_____

_____

18 Find and copy four aims of the UK Zoo Licensing Act 1981. **(3 marks)**
Focus: Describe, select and retrieve information and events or ideas from the text. Use quotation and reference to the text.

_____

_____

_____

_____

_____

_____

_____

_____

_____

_____

_____

19

In the last 20 years, UK zoos have had to contend with growing levels of public scepticism and concern as more and more people question their justification.

Explain the meaning of 'public scepticism' from this context. **(2 marks)**

Focus: Deduce, infer and interpret information and events or ideas from the text.

_____

_____

_____

_____

_____

_____

_____

_____

_____

_____

20 Quote two words which show that the Official Zoo Health Check 2000 is something whose views and opinions you can trust. **(3 marks)**

Focus: Identify and comment on the writer's purposes and viewpoints, and the effect of the text on the reader.

_____

_____

_____

_____

_____

_____

_____

_____

_____

_____

21 How does the use of diagrams and other organisational features on this website page help you
   to understand and believe the words of the Official Zoo Health Check 2000?   **(2 marks)**
   Focus: Comment on the structure and organisation of texts, grammatical and presentational features at text level.

_____

_____

_____

_____

_____

_____

_____

_____

_____

_____

_____

22 Explain the reasons for the writer's use of the following punctuation marks.   **(3 marks)**
   Focus: Comment on the writer's use of language, grammatical and literary features at word and sentence level.

Brackets	open to the public seven or more days in 12 consecutive months (UK Zoo Licensing Act 1981)
Quotation marks	reports to be published on the 'health' of UK zoos
Equals sign	**SZ** = Small Zoo **W** = Wildlife/Safari Park

_____

_____

_____

_____

_____

_____

_____

_____

_____

_____

The way we treat animals

These two writing assignments are linked to the theme of 'The way we treat animals'.

Major task

- You should spend about 40 minutes on this.
- There are 30 marks available.

Write a speech to be delivered in a debate, putting forward the motion that all experimentation on animals is cruel and ought to be banned.

Think about these points:
- Whom are you addressing?
- Each of your arguments needs to be backed up.
- Make up some statistics if necessary.
- What kind of style is necessary in a debate?
- What kind of stylistic features will you need to use?

Planning notes:
- Before you start writing, use the format on this page to help you to plan and write notes.
- Allow time to read your work and check your use of language before you finish.

Introduction Ladies and gentlemen … Say what you believe	**The personal touch** Make the audience feel they understand the situation You all know about … You will all have heard about …
Argument 1	**Facts to back it up**
Argument 2 **Argument 3** Facts to back them up	**Conclusion** Sum up the arguments Appeal to the humanity and good sense of the audience

Minor task

- You should spend about 25 minutes on this.
- There are 20 marks available.

Imagine you are going away and have to leave your pet in the hands of someone you do not know. Write a brief report on how to look after the pet.

You should write only three paragraphs to:
- inform the reader
- ensure that the layout of the report makes understanding easier.

Do not use the same information as you included in your answer to the major writing task.

Planning notes:
- Before you start writing, use the format on this page to help you to plan and write notes.
- Organise your ideas into three paragraphs only.
- Allow time to read your work and check your use of language before you finish.

Daily routine	Feeding
Keeping the animal healthy	**Exercise**
Sleeping arrangements	**Things which could go wrong**

Train journeys

The theme linking these three reading texts is 'Train journeys'.
- You have 1 hour and 15 minutes to answer the questions on the three passages.
- You are given 15 minutes' reading time before this.

Reading test 1

Reading and interpreting a passage from *Just William on Holiday* by Richmal Crompton

William sat alone in the railway carriage and watched telegraph poles, cows and trees fly past the window. He was mildly interested in the sight and amused himself by pretending that it was the train that was stationary and the surrounding countryside that was moving.

Mrs Brown had gone into a nursing home for a slight operation, and, in order to relieve the domestic strain, William was being sent to stay with an old school friend of hers, who lived at a small seaside resort called Sea Beach.

He was enjoying the journey. He always enjoyed journeys. He enjoyed the motion and the change from the ordinary routine of life. They had a generally exhilarating effect on him, and he could, of course, enliven them by pretending that he was anyone going anywhere.

Since the journey began he had pretended that he was a spy travelling disguised through an enemy country (none of the other people in the carriage suspected him), a general on his way to the war (the other people in the carriage were his staff), and a circus man travelling with his show (the large man with the long nose was an elephant and the woman in the black satin coat was a performing seal).

All the other passengers had got out at various stations, and now William was alone, pretending to be a wizard, who, by a wave of his wand, made trees, fields, telegraph posts skip to his bidding.

After a few minutes he tired of this; he was growing slightly bored. Suddenly his eye lit on the notice: "To stop the train, pull down the chain."

He stretched out his hand to it, then read: "Penalty for improper use, £5", and, after a hasty mental calculation that assessed his entire capital at the sum of one shilling and sixpence halfpenny, put his hand down again.

But the fascination of it was more than he could resist. He fingered the chain, and imagined himself pulling it. He wondered if it really worked and, if it worked, how it worked. It probably put on a sort of brake. There wouldn't be any harm in just pulling it a tiny bit. That would only just make the train go a little bit more slowly. No one would even notice it.

He pulled the chain an infinitesimal fraction.

Nothing happened.

He pulled it a little harder.

Still nothing happened.

He pulled it harder still. There was a sudden screaming of brakes, and the train drew to an abrupt standstill.

William crouched in his corner of the carriage, frozen with horror. Perhaps, he thought desperately, if he sat quite still and didn't move or breathe, they wouldn't know who'd done it.

The guard came running down by the side of the train*. As he approached William's carriage, an elderly, red-faced, military-looking gentleman leant out of the

* In those days there were no doorways between the separate carriages on trains.

next window, and gasped: "Guard, guard! You're in the nick of time", then poured out an incoherent story about a man who had demanded money from him, and was just raising his stick to brain him when the train stopped.

"Then, of course, he jumped and escaped," he ended. "Look! There he is!"

The figure of a large but nimble man could be seen disappearing across a field on the other side of the train. Immediately outside the carriage was the stick that he had evidently thrown away in his flight.

"Just in time, guard," panted the military-looking man, mopping his brow. "Another minute, and – "

William heaved a sigh of relief. No one would now know that it was he who had pulled the chain.

"But you didn't pull the chain, sir," the guard was saying.

"No, the brute was standing right over me, so that I couldn't move. He – "

"The chain was pulled from this carriage," went on the guard, moving towards William, who sat in his corner, frozen by horror once more, trying to efface himself against the carriage back.

The guard stood and looked at him for a few seconds in silence, then he said:

"That was smart work of yours, nipper. I suppose, sir," he went on, turning to the military-looking man, "he heard this fellow threatening you and pulled the chain."

William, after a few seconds' complete bewilderment, clutched gratefully at this heaven-sent deliverance.

The military-looking man shook hands with him, thanked him effusively, and gave him a ten shilling note. The other passengers came up and crowded round him, wringing his hand and congratulating him. An old lady gave him a peppermint drop. A little girl produced an autograph album and asked for his signature.

William, though still somewhat bewildered, assumed an air of modest heroism.

Finally, the guard, having taken all the particulars of his adventure from the military-looking man, sent everyone back to their carriage, and the train started once more on its way.

William, alone in his carriage, felt at first merely a great relief at his providential rescue from ignominy. Then gradually the imaginary scene became more and more real. He saw himself starting up at the sound of a fierce altercation from the next carriage, then coming to a sudden decision and dashing to the chain. He sat for the rest of the journey smiling modestly to himself, bathed in a roseate glow of heroism.

His hostess, Mrs Beacon, met him at the station. She was a large, placid woman who, William decided at once, would probably be amenable but uninteresting. He hoped that she would realise that he was a hero. He meant to lose no time in telling her the story.

But it wasn't even necessary to tell it to her, for it turned out that several of the passengers were coming to Sea Beach, and they crowded round William once more, recounting his exploit to his hostess and congratulating him.

William's modest but heroic smile intensified. He depreciated his exploit with airy gestures.

"Oh, it was nothin'," he said; "it jus' sort o' seemed the only thing to do. It was nothin' at all really."

But Sea Beach didn't appear to think it was nothing at all. There had been a complete dearth of local news for several months, and it seized on William with avidity.

Its local paper sent a reporter to interview him and printed his portrait on its first page under the heading: Our Boy Hero. People pointed him out to each other as he walked along the promenade, wearing his modest but heroic smile.

Questions 1–8 are about *Just William on Holiday*

1   Copy and quote three clauses which express William's irresistible fascination with the train's communication cord.   **(1 mark)**
    Focus: Describe, select and retrieve information and events or ideas from the text. Use quotation and reference to the text.

_____

_____

_____

_____

_____

_____

_____

2   Give two examples from the passage which show that William has a strong imagination. **(1 mark)**
    Focus: Describe, select and retrieve information and events or ideas from the text. Use quotation and reference to the text.

_____

_____

_____

_____

_____

_____

_____

3   Explain in your own words what made William pull the train's communication cord.   **(1 mark)**
    Focus: Deduce, infer and interpret information and events or ideas from the text.

_____

_____

_____

_____

_____

_____

_____

_____

4   How does the writer express how William felt after he pulled the communication cord? **(2 marks)**
    Focus: Comment on the writer's use of language, grammatical and literary features at word and sentence level.

    _____

    _____

    _____

    _____

    _____

    _____

    _____

5   Explain William's bewilderment at what happened after he pulled the communication cord.
    (2 marks)

    Focus: Deduce, infer and interpret information and events or ideas from the text.

    _____

    _____

    _____

    _____

    _____

    _____

    _____

    _____

6   List in chronological order the key events which took place on the train.   **(3 marks)**
    Focus: Describe, select and retrieve information and events or ideas from the text. Use quotation and reference to the text.

    _____

    _____

    _____

    _____

    _____

    _____

    _____

7   Summarise the first three paragraphs of the passage and explain their purpose.   **(3 marks)**
    Focus: Comment on the structure and organisation of texts, grammatical and presentational features at text level.

_____

_____

_____

_____

_____

_____

_____

_____

_____

_____

_____

_____

8   How does the writer communicate William's changing emotions throughout the journey?
    You should write about:
    ● what William felt at different points in the journey, and why
    ● the language used to communicate these feelings; note any interesting figures of speech,
      verbs, adjectives, nouns and adverbs
    ● the mild and strong emotions and explain how they are expressed.   **(4 marks)**
    Focus: Identify and comment on the writer's purposes and viewpoints, and the effect of the text on the reader.

_____

_____

_____

_____

_____

_____

_____

_____

_____

_____

_____

Reading test 2
Reading and interpreting a poem by Edward Thomas

Adlestrop

Yes. I remember Adlestrop –
The name, because one afternoon
Of heat the express-train drew up there
Unwontedly. It was late June.

The steam hissed. Someone cleared his throat.
No one left and no one came
On the bare platform. What I saw
Was Adlestrop – only the name

And willows, willow-herb, and grass,
And meadowsweet, and haycocks dry,
No whit less still and lonely fair
Than the high cloudlets in the sky.

And for that minute a blackbird sang
Close by, and round him, mistier,
Farther and farther, all the birds
Of Oxfordshire and Gloucestershire.

Questions 9–16 are about *Adlestrop*

9 List three sounds which the poet heard at Adlestrop.   **(1 mark)**
   Focus: Describe, select and retrieve information and events or ideas from the text. Use quotation and reference to the text.

_____

_____

_____

_____

10 What evidence can you find to show that, although it is short, this is a narrative as well as a
   descriptive poem?   **(2 marks)**
   Focus: Comment on the structure and organisation of texts, grammatical and presentational features at text level.

_____

_____

_____

_____

11 Describe Adlestrop and support your answer with quotations from the text. **(1 mark)**
   Focus: Describe, select and retrieve information and events or ideas from the text. Use quotation and reference to the text.

_____

_____

_____

_____

_____

_____

_____

_____

_____

_____

_____

_____

_____

_____

12 Explain the effect on the reader of the writer's use of sentences which end in the middle of
   a line. **(3 marks)**
   Focus: Comment on the structure and organisation of texts, grammatical and presentational features at text level.

_____

_____

_____

_____

_____

_____

_____

_____

_____

_____

_____

13 What image does this line conjure up in your mind? **(2 marks)**

> No whit less still and lonely fair …

Focus: Comment on the writer's use of language, grammatical and literary features at word and sentence level.

_____

_____

_____

_____

_____

_____

_____

_____

_____

_____

_____

14 List the words in the poem which suggest the emptiness of the station at Adlestrop. **(2 marks)**
Focus: Comment on the writer's use of language, grammatical and literary features at word and sentence level.

_____

_____

_____

_____

_____

_____

_____

_____

_____

_____

_____

15 What do you notice about the rhythm and pace of the poem and how this is created through the syllable-patterns of the words, the length of lines and the rhyme pattern? **(3 marks)**
Focus: Comment on the structure and organisation of texts, grammatical and presentational features at text level.

_____

_____

_____

_____

_____

_____

_____

_____

_____

_____

16 Describe the atmosphere of the station at Adlestrop and explain how the poet creates this atmosphere.
You should write about:
● the scene conjured up in your mind, including the sounds
● what you feel is the atmosphere
● how the poet uses rhythm to create atmosphere
● the poet's choice of words. **(5 marks)**
Focus: Identify and comment on the writer's purposes and viewpoints, and the effect of the text on the reader.

_____

_____

_____

_____

_____

_____

_____

_____

_____

_____

Reading test 3
Reading and interpreting *the website of National Rail*

The home page of National Rail

Each icon below can be used to reach other pages of the website.

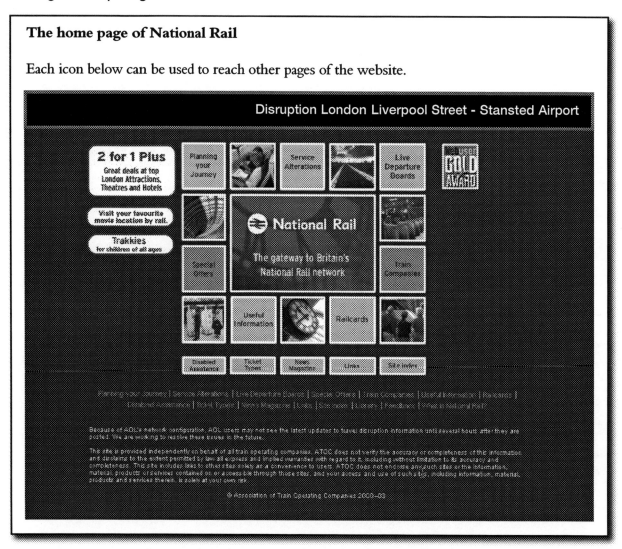

The page which follows (http://www.nationalrail.co.uk/info/fs_info.htm) was obtained by clicking on 'Useful Information'.

Users can click on any of the icons on the page in order to reach other pages.

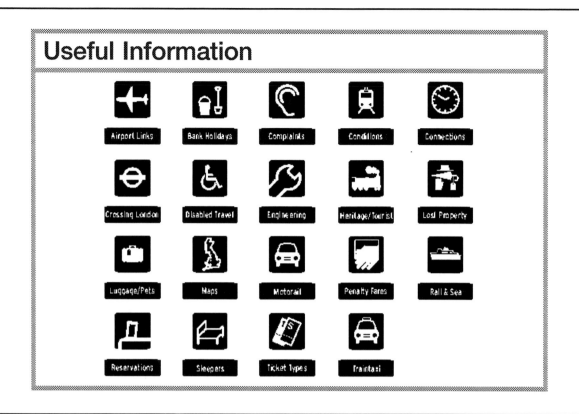

Useful Information

Airport Links	Bank Holidays	Complaints	Conditions	Connections
Crossing London	Disabled Travel	Engineering	Heritage/Tourist	Lost Property
Luggage/Pets	Maps	Motorail	Penalty Fares	Rail & Sea
Reservations	Sleepers	Ticket Types	Traintaxi	

Below are some of the pages which can be reached by clicking on some of the icons above. These, in turn, can be used to reach other pages.

Passengers Needing Special Assistance

Help us to help you

Special arrangements can be made for disabled or mobility-impaired passengers. For example, we can usually arrange for staff to meet you at your departure station, accompany you to the train and see you safely on board. Similar arrangements can be made at your destination station and other stations if you need to change trains.

- Contact the train company for your starting station.

- If you are uncertain which train company this is, you can find out here.

- If you already know the name of the train company, contact details (including mobility-impaired helpline and minicom/textphone) are available here.

- We are more able to help you if you contact us as far in advance as possible. Please try to give at least 24 hours' notice of your journey. If you do not give us notice, we will try to help but cannot guarantee to provide the normal level of service.

- Information on the Disabled Persons Railcard is available here.

- The booklet "Rail Travel for Disabled Passengers" is available for download here.

Choosing Your Rail Ticket

If you are unsure about which rail ticket is best for your journey, phone National Rail Enquiries on **08457 48 49 50** or contact Train Company information sources.

Details of the Train Companies – together with links to their web sites, where appropriate – are also available from the Train Companies section of this site.

Return to top

What Ticket Suits You Best

The following summary shows when you can buy rail tickets, and when you can use these tickets within the periods of time for which they are valid. When you are planning a journey, use this guide to help you to choose the best ticket for your needs. You can get advice and full details about the wide range of tickets available and when you can use them, from rail information staff.

Buy Anytime, Travel Anytime
You can buy fully-flexible tickets at any time, with no limits on travel, and they let you travel at any time during the period they are valid. These include Open and some Day tickets. They're ideal for business travellers and anyone else who needs to travel at the busiest times, for example, rush hour.

Buy Anytime, Travel Restricted
You can often buy cheaper tickets by accepting some limits on when you can travel. Look out for tickets such as SuperSavers, Savers, Cheap Day Returns and, in London and the South East, AwayBreaks.

Buy In Advance, Travel Anytime
On a few routes, you can buy tickets in advance which let you travel at any time during the period they are valid.

Buy In Advance, Specified Trains
You can buy bargain tickets, in advance, on many routes. Many of these tickets include a free seat reservation but they **are only available in limited numbers, and at certain times, on specific trains**. If you can plan your journey and buy your ticket at least one day in advance (or for some advance tickets, several days in advance), these tickets are excellent value for money.

Multi-journey
You can buy Season Tickets and multi-modal tickets that give you unlimited travel on certain routes and in certain areas. Season tickets are valid for seven days, or for any period from a month to a year.

Special Tickets
Train Companies often offer other tickets, including special bargain tickets, which may be more suitable for your journey needs. You can: visit staffed stations; contact National Rail Enquiries **(08457 48 49 50)**; or visit Train Company Internet sites; for more information.

You can get discounts on many services if there are 10 or more of you travelling together, **when you book in advance**. You can also get smaller group-discount tickets on some services, if less than 10 of you are travelling.

You can get Regional Rover tickets in some areas. The All-Line Rover ticket gives you excellent value for money for seven or 14 days of unlimited National Rail network travel throughout Great Britain.

The above list is a summary of ticket choices. You can get full information on tickets, when you can use them and other conditions that apply to them from rail information staff.

Questions 17–22 are about *the website of National Rail*

17 In what three ways do rail staff offer assistance to mobility-impaired or disabled passengers at their departure station? **(1 mark)**
Focus: Describe, select and retrieve information and events or ideas from the text. Use quotation and reference to the text.

_____

_____

_____

_____

_____

_____

_____

18 Select three icons on the 'Useful Information' page on which you would click to help you to plan a journey on a weekday from your home to London (or, if you live in London, to Edinburgh), and say what kind of information you hope to find on each page. **(3 marks)**
Focus: Describe, select and retrieve information and events or ideas from the text. Use quotation and reference to the text.

_____

_____

_____

_____

_____

_____

_____

19 List three factors which affect the price of rail tickets. **(2 marks)**
Focus: Deduce, infer and interpret information and events or ideas from the text.

_____

_____

_____

_____

_____

_____

20 Identify an example in the passage of the use of each of the following punctuation marks and explain why they are used: brackets, bullets and dashes. **(2 marks)**
Focus: Comment on the writer's use of language, grammatical and literary features at word and sentence level.

_____

_____

_____

_____

_____

_____

_____

21 How well does the heading 'Choosing Your Rail Ticket' describe the page from which the information in the passage was taken, and how would you improve it? **(3 marks)**
Focus: Comment on the structure and organisation of texts, grammatical and presentational features at text level.

_____

_____

_____

_____

_____

_____

_____

22 How does the use of icons and other organisational features on this website help users to find the information they want?
You should comment on:
● the ways in which the website helps users to identify quickly the pages they need
● the use of web devices to help users to move easily from one page to another
● the use of bold, different fonts and other layout devices. **(3 marks)**
Focus: Identify and comment on the writer's purposes and viewpoints, and the effect of the text on the reader.

_____

_____

_____

_____

_____

_____

Train journeys

These two writing assignments are linked to the theme of 'Train journeys'.

Major task

- You should spend about 40 minutes on this.
- There are 30 marks available.

Write a promotional text advertising rail travel and persuading travellers that it is better than other forms of transport.

Think about these points:
- What are the advantages of rail travel?
- What are the disadvantages of other modes of transport?
- What image of rail travel do you want to create?
- How will this image appeal to different types of traveller? (Consider the reasons why people travel.)
- What persuasive words and phrases will you use?

Planning notes:
- Before you start writing, use the format on this page to help you to plan and write notes.
- Allow time to read your work and check your use of language before you finish.

Introduction Attract the attention of readers Make rail travel sound appealing	
Advantages of rail travel	**Disadvantages of other modes of transport**
The image of rail travel	**Conclusion** Sum up what rail travel offers to the traveller
Useful words and phrases	

Minor task

- You should spend about 25 minutes on this.
- There are 20 marks available.

Write a letter to a rail company to complain about the condition of one of their trains on which you have travelled.

You should write a paragraph for each of the following:
- to explain why you are writing the letter and giving details of your journey
- to describe what was wrong with the train and the journey
- to sum up (say what you hope the letter will achieve).

Planning notes:
- Before you start writing, use the format on this page to help you to plan and write notes.
- Organise your ideas into three paragraphs.
- Allow time to read your work and check your use of language before you finish.

Introductory paragraph
Reason for writing the letter
Details of your journey (starting point, destination and time)

The complaint
The points which spoiled your journey

Summary
What you hope will be achieved by the letter

Answers to Test Paper 7: Storms

Questions 1–7 are about *The Great Storm of 1987*

1   Find and copy three effects of the storm.   **(2 marks)**
    Focus: Describe, select and retrieve information and events or ideas from the text. Use quotation and reference to the text.
    15 million trees were lost. Trees blocked roads and railways and brought down electricity and telephone lines. Hundreds of thousands of homes in England remained without power for more than 24 hours. Falling trees and masonry damaged or destroyed buildings and cars. Numerous small boats were wrecked or blown away. A ship capsized at Dover, and a Channel ferry was driven ashore near Folkestone. The storm killed 18 people in England and at least four in France.

2   Explain why 'The death toll might have been far greater had the storm struck in the daytime'.   **(2 marks)**
    Focus: Deduce, infer and interpret information and events or ideas from the text
    At night there are fewer people around, fewer cars on the road, and so on. The damage caused would have been greater because more people would have been affected.

3   Say what you think 'equivocal', used earlier in the sentence, might mean from reading the following sentence.
    Focus: Deduce, infer and interpret information and events or ideas from the text.   **(2 marks)**

Instead of stormy weather over a considerable part of the UK, the models suggested that severe weather would reach no farther north than the English Channel and coastal parts of southern England.

    The word means 'capable of having more than one interpretation'. In this sense the weather forecasters did not really know what was going to happen, so they gave more than one possible occurrence to be on the safe side. This tended to underestimate the severity of the storm.

4   Select and quote three examples of technical language about the subject which show that this comes from the website of an official organisation.   **(2 marks)**
    Focus: Describe, select and retrieve information and events or ideas from the text. Use quotation and reference to the text.
    'The pressure gradient was slack.' 'A depression was drifting slowly northwards over the North Sea off eastern Scotland.' 'A col lay over England, Wales and Ireland.' 'Over the Bay of Biscay, a depression was developing.'

5   Comment on the reasons for the different uses of dashes and hyphens in the following examples.   **(2 marks)**
    Focus: Comment on the writer's use of language, grammatical and literary features at word and sentence level.

This storm, he said, would not reach the British Isles – and it didn't. The Great Storm of 1987 did not originate in the Tropics and was not, by any definition, a hurricane – but it was certainly exceptional.	South-east of a line extending from Southampton … A 10-minute mean wind speed of 70 knots …

    Dashes separate ideas. In the first examples, they allow the writer to stop what he was saying in the sentence and to add more information.
    Hyphens join ideas or words, so 'south' and 'east' become one compound adjective in 'south-east'.

6   Write the events of the passage in a time chart.   **(2 marks)**
    Focus: Comment on the structure and organisation of texts, grammatical and presentational features at text level.

Four or five days before	*Bad weather predicted the following week*
Afternoon of 15 October	*Wind slight*
Evening of 15 October	*Some mention of strong winds but more mention of heavy rain*
16 October	*Warning of severe storm*

7   The writer has to explain that the storm was very serious but that it was not a 'hurricane' in the scientific
    sense. How successful is he?   **(4 marks)**
    Focus: Comment on the writer's use of language, grammatical and literary features at word and sentence level.
    Much of the information required for this answer will have been deduced from earlier questions.
    *Michael Fish was referring to a tropical cyclone and not the hurricane, so he was not wrong. The writer gives
    us the scientific definition of a hurricane in terms of wind speed. In most cases over the country the speed
    was not reached, so this was not officially a hurricane. The writer divides the information into sections with
    subheadings to make it easier to read, and uses technical vocabulary but tries to explain the terms used.*

Questions 8–14 are about *Wind*

8   Quote two examples of personification from the first verse.   **(2 marks)**
    Focus: Describe, select and retrieve information and events or ideas from the text. Use quotation and reference to the text.
    *The **woods crashing** through darkness, the booming hills, / **Wind stampeding** the fields under the windows*

9   State which verbs are used to describe the actions of both. Explain how these show the effect of the storm.
                                                                                                    (2 marks)
    Focus: Deduce, infer and interpret information and events or ideas from the text.
    *'Crashing': this is an onomatopoeic (sound) word. It suggests the noise of the trees in the storm. It is as if
    they were running through the woods, clumsily bumping into things.*
    'Stampeding': suggests speed and destruction, as if the trees were a group of people out of control.

10 What impression does the onomatopoeic adjective 'booming' (line 2) give of the effect of the storm on the
    countryside?   **(1 mark)**
    Focus: Comment on the writer's use of language, grammatical and literary features at word and sentence level.
    *The word suggests the sound of the storm. It is a deep, echoing sound and suggests that the sounds come
    from a great distance. It is as if the storm is huge and frightening.*

11 Look carefully at the structure of the poem. Using the chart write in the numbers of the verses which deal
    with the world *outside* and the world *inside*.   **(2 marks)**
    Focus: Comment on the structure and organisation of texts, grammatical and presentational features at text level.

Verses describing outside	Verses describing inside
1, 2, 3, 4	*5, 6*

12 'The wind flung a magpie away, and a black / Back gull bent like an iron bar slowly.'
    a. What does the verb 'flung' tell the reader about the storm?
    b. Explain how the simile 'bent like an iron bar' creates an effective image of a bird flying in the face of
       a storm.   **(2 marks)**
    Focus: Comment on the writer's use of language, grammatical and literary features at word and sentence level.
    *'Flung' is a very violent word. It is as if the bird is being thrown by the wind – it is in its control. It also
    suggests speed and lack of control.*
    *'Bent like an iron bar' suggests the way in which the bird is fighting the wind and struggles. An iron bar is
    very difficult to bend and it can only be done very slowly. The poet sees the bird slowly giving up its struggle
    against the wind and being forced violently into a contorted shape.*

13 In the last two verses of the poem, the writer considers the effects of the storm on people in the house. Find
    words the poet uses to give an impression of their state of mind: for example, why are they 'deep in their
    chairs'? Why do they 'grip their hearts'?
    Look at what they are doing, what this means and the way this is described.   **(2 marks)**
    Focus: Comment on the writer's use of language, grammatical and literary features at word and sentence level.
    'Now deep / In chairs ... we grip / Our hearts and cannot entertain book, thought, / Or each other.'
    *The people in the house express their fear of the strength of the elements outside. They huddle deeper into
    their chairs to hide; they are silent because they are afraid – it is as if they are clutching hold of their hearts
    to slow down the beat. They cannot look at one another or do anything because they are so afraid.*

14 Ted Hughes is known as a very 'physical' poet: readers can feel through their senses what it would have been like to experience the storm. How successfully do you think he has created this effect in 'Wind'?

(5 marks)

Focus: Comment on the writer's purposes and viewpoints, and the effect of the text on the reader.
Many of the answers already given will provide valuable information for this answer.
The entire poem appeals to our senses. We are made to see, hear and feel the power of the storm. The imagery is very violent, reflecting the storm. The imagery is also very physical: for example, the gull being bent 'like an iron bar'.

Questions 15–22 are about *The Night the Water Came*

15 Find and copy two signs which showed Apu that the storm was approaching. (2 marks)
Focus: Describe, select and retrieve information and events or ideas from the text. Use quotation and reference to the text.
'I could hear the wind blowing hard and roaring in the branches of the tree.'
'I couldn't even see the stars, so the sky must have been covered with clouds.'

16 Explain why the writer uses brackets in the following two examples. (2 marks)
'(I mean, it used to stand there. I still can't get used to the idea that it's gone.)'
'(I mean he used to, he's not there any more.)'
Focus: Comment on the writer's use of language, grammatical and literary features at word and sentence level.
The narrator realises that these things existed before the storm. This tells the reader that the narrator survived the experience and is telling the story later.

17 Why did it seem like 'an odd time to be climbing trees'? (2 marks)
Focus: Describe, select and retrieve information and events or ideas from the text. Use quotation and reference to the text.
He had been dragged from his bed at night. Climbing trees is usually a daytime play activity.

18 Describe and explain the reasons for the different reactions of the adults and Apu as the storm approached.

(2 marks)

Focus: Deduce, infer and interpret information and events or ideas from the text.
Apu does as he is told and, as he is used to climbing trees, this just seems like a big adventure. The adults cannot believe that the storm will be so bad and so do not do as they are told. They are not used to climbing trees and so this seems a very childish and ridiculous thing to do.

19 '… but suddenly there was something darker and blacker flying through the air like a huge bat and wrapping itself round the lower branches of my tree.' What was Apu describing? Show how the writer's use of the simile helps us to imagine the scene better. (2 marks)
Focus: Comment on the writer's use of language, grammatical and literary features at word and sentence level.
Apu is describing the thatch from his roof which has been blown away in the storm. The simile gives us an impression of a huge dark silhouette in a ragged shape, flying erratically around – just as bats would do. We cannot imagine such a roof being blown away, so the writer finds a visual way of fixing the image in our minds.

20 List two verbs used to describe the impact of the water and explain how they add to the impression of the storm. (2 marks)
Focus: Comment on the writer's use of language, grammatical and literary features at word and sentence level.
'Roaring': onomatopoeic – it shows the strength of the flood which followed the storm.
'Rushing': onomatopoeic – it shows the speed of the water.

21 How do we know that the tree containing Apu fell into the water from the sea? (1 mark)
Focus: Deduce, infer and interpret information and events or ideas from the text.
He lives on an island. The water was salty.

Answers: Test Paper 7

22 Apu writes in a first-person narrative. How important is this to the author's intention of showing us the ferocity of the storm and what it would have been like to be at the centre of it? **(5 marks)**

Focus: Identify and comment on the writer's purposes and viewpoints, and the effect of the text on the reader.

Many of the responses to previous questions in this unit can be incorporated here.

A first-person narration is always more personal because we see the world through the eyes of one person. We get personal responses to situations and we learn how the person feels. We often sympathise with the feelings of a person. The boy gives us a child's innocent view of the coming of the storm. He climbs the tree on instructions, but has no concept that everyone else will die. He does not appear to be afraid – he is too concerned with clinging to the tree to stay alive.

Test Paper 7 Mark scheme: Questions and assessment focuses

Question	Focus and number of marks (G: includes a focus on grammar)				
	Describe, select and retrieve information and events or ideas from the text. Use quotation and reference to the text.	Deduce, infer and interpret information and events or ideas from the text.	Comment on the structure and organisation of texts, grammatical and presentational features at text level.	Comment on the writer's use of language, grammatical and literary features at word and sentence level.	Identify and comment on the writer's purposes and viewpoints, and the effect of the text on the reader.
1:1	2				
1:2		2			
1:3		2			
1:4	2				
1:5				2	
1:6			2 G		
1:7				4	
2:8	2				
2:9		2 G			
2:10				1	
2:11			2		
2:12				2	
2:13				2	
2:14					5
3:15	2				
3:16				2 G	
3:17	2				
3:18		2			
3:19				2	
3:20				2	
3:21		1			
3:22					5
Total	**10**	**9**	**4**	**17**	**10**

Answers to Test Paper 8: The way we treat animals

Questions 1–8 are about *The Rats of NIMH*

1 Quote the verb used in the first sentence which gives us the impression of what the movement was like when being carried in a net. **(1 mark)**
Focus: Describe, select and retrieve information and events or ideas from the text. Use quotation and reference to the text.
'Swinging back and forth'.

2 Find and copy two things which the narrator noticed about the inside of the van. **(2 marks)**
Focus: Describe, select and retrieve information and events or ideas from the text. Use quotation and reference to the text.
'Interior was a large wire cage', 'The floor … was covered with sawdust'.

3 Explain in your own words how the rats felt about being captured in this way. **(1 mark)**
Focus: Deduce, infer and interpret information and events or ideas from the text.
They did not understand what was happening to them ('dazed') and they were very afraid of this strange situation ('terrified').

4 Look at the passages of speech. How does the reader know which of the characters is speaking? **(2 marks)**
Focus: Comment on the writer's use of language, grammatical and literary features at word and sentence level.
The speech does not have names of characters after the speeches. This does not make any difference to our understanding because we know that each new speaker in direct speech should be written on a new line, therefore each character must speak in turn. We are given an indication at first that either Jenner or Nicodemus speaks and we can then work it out.

5 Explain why 'You can imagine how glad I was to hear him. But I was sorry, too'. **(2 marks)**
Focus: Deduce, infer and interpret information and events or ideas from the text.
Nicodemus was pleased to hear a friendly voice in the van to show that he was not alone, but he was sorry because the other rat had been captured as well.

6 List the details you are given about the building to which the rats were taken. What feelings does this description evoke in the reader? **(3 marks)**
Focus: Describe, select and retrieve information and events or ideas from the text. Use quotation and reference to the text.
The laboratory is described very factually and coldly: modern … white cement … glass … square … big … windows were dark …
There is no emotion attached to the description, which is an indication of the kind of experimentation which goes on inside it. It is a characterless building – no colour or features to make it special. This makes the reader somewhat wary of it.

7 Quote two examples to show that this is a first-person narrative. How does using a first-person narrative make us feel more sympathetic towards the character? **(2 marks)**
Focus: Comment on the writer's use of language, grammatical and literary features at word and sentence level.
'I felt myself being lifted', 'You can imagine how glad I was …'.
First-person narrations always give us a more personal view and here we can sympathise more with the situation of the captured animal. We feel and think along with him. When the rat describes what it is like we can understand the images he is using.

8 'That cage was my home for a long time.' Explain the rat's attitude towards the cage and how the author's description makes the reader feel. **(4 marks)**
Focus: Identify and comment on the writer's purposes and viewpoints, and the effect of the text on the reader.
The cage was not uncomfortable, but any cage restricts and the rat had been used to running free wherever he wanted. Even though all bodily needs were taken care of, the animal was still a prisoner. The cage made him feel at the mercy of someone else and uncertain of what would happen next. Experimentation was associated with the cage and this can hint at cruelty.

Answers: Test Paper 8

Questions 9–16 are about *The Caged Bird in Springtime*

9 In verse 1, the bird is curious about a new feeling. What is it? **(1 mark)**
   Focus: Describe, select and retrieve information and events or ideas from the text. Use quotation and reference to the text.
   The bird feels as if it does not want to be caged any more but wants to fly away and be free.

10 What evidence can you find to show that this is a first-person narration? **(1mark)**
   Focus: Comment on the structure and organisation of texts, grammatical and presentational features at text level.
   'As if I wanted ...', 'I have never flown ...', 'Though I have heard ...'.

11 Say what you think is the subject of each verse, and how the poet introduces this in the first line of
   each verse. **(4 marks)**
   Focus: Comment on the structure and organisation of texts, grammatical and presentational features at text level.

Verse	Subject	First line quotation
1	*Sudden new feeling – nor wanting to be caged*	*What can it be ...?*
2	*Does not know what flying is*	*But how absurd!*
3	*Wanting to do what free birds do*	*Why do I peck the wires of this little cage?*
4	*Realises that being outside the cage is the only way to be free*	*I cannot quite remember how ...*
5	*Singing is a sign of real sadness*	*I have all I need ...*

12 Explain the effect on the reader of the use of the adjectives in the following descriptions:
   'this *little* cage ...', 'these *sharp* wires...'. **(3 marks)**
   Focus: Comment on the writer's use of language, grammatical and literary features at word and sentence level.
   *They show how the life of the bird has been restricted and make us feel sorry for it. 'Little' shows how
   restricted it is. Birds are normally free to fly where they like. This cage is the bird's whole world.
   'Sharp' makes the cage sound even more cruel. The bird is beating its head against the wires, so this image
   is one of pain. The bird is so frustrated that it is trying to get out.*

13 Explain the metaphor 'the secret branches of the air' and its effect. **(2 marks)**
   Focus: Comment on the writer's use of language, grammatical and literary features at word and sentence level.
   *The bird imagines a tree outside the cage, but as it has never been outside it cannot really imagine a real
   tree. It feels that the air itself has branches – hence 'secret'.*

14 When the bird says, 'I have all I need', explain why this is not the case. **(2 marks)**
   Focus: Deduce, infer and interpret information and events or ideas from the text.
   *The bird has all the elements to survive according to human beings, but in fact it only wants its freedom,
   which the humans will not allow.*

15 '... Against these sharp wires, while the children / Smile at each other, saying: 'Hark how he sings''. Explain
   the real reason for the bird's singing and how the children's misconception about the bird makes you feel.
   (2 marks)
   Focus: Deduce, infer and interpret information and events or ideas from the text.
   *The children think the bird is singing because it is happy in its cage. They do not know the real feelings of
   the bird. It is desperately unhappy and is in fact struggling to get out. The final image is a very cruel one
   and the reader probably feels a little guilty.*

16 How do you feel about the bird in the cage? **(4 marks)**
   Focus: Identify and comment on the writer's purposes and viewpoints, and the effect of the text on the reader.
   *All the information necessary for this answer has been provided in other questions. The pupils should be
   reorganising and structuring the information accordingly. The question asks for a personal response and as
   long as this can be backed up realistically from the text, any view should be rewarded.*

Questions 17–22 are about *UK Zoos: Fit for life?*

17 'In the UK, an estimated $\frac{1}{4}$ million animals – large and small – are held in more than 400 zoological collections*.' Explain the purpose of the asterisk. **(1 mark)**
   Focus: Comment on the writer's use of language, grammatical and literary features at word and sentence level.
   The asterisk indicates to the reader that there is further information to be found on the page where the asterisk is to be found.

18 Find and copy four aims of the UK Zoo Licensing Act 1981. **(3 marks)**
   Focus: Describe, select and retrieve information and events or ideas from the text. Use quotation and reference to the text.
   'To promote minimum standards of welfare, meaningful education, effective conservation, valuable research and essential public safety.'

19 'In the last 20 years, UK zoos have had to contend with growing levels of public scepticism and concern as more and more people question their justification.' Explain the meaning of 'public scepticism' from this context.
   (2 marks)
   Focus: Deduce, infer and interpret information and events or ideas from the text.
   This word suggests that, despite what they have been told, the public does not believe the official view of what zoos do.

20 Quote two words which show that the Official Zoo Health Check 2000 is something whose views and opinions you can trust. **(3 marks)**
   Focus: Identify and comment on the writer's purposes and viewpoints, and the effect of the text on the reader.
   *'The first of a series of **independent** and **comprehensive** zoo investigations by a team of scientists from the **renowned** international wildlife charity ...'*

21 How does the use of diagrams and other organisational features on this website page help you to understand and believe the words of the Official Zoo Health Check 2000? **(2 marks)**
   Focus: Comment on the structure and organisation of texts, grammatical and presentational features at text level.
   The charts and boxed text help readers to see and understand sections of more difficult information. They break down the statistics so that they become visual.

22 Explain the reasons for the writer's use of the following punctuation marks. **(3 marks)**
   Focus: Comment on the writer's use of language, grammatical and literary features at word and sentence level.

Brackets	open to the public seven or more days in 12 consecutive months (UK Zoo Licensing Act 1981)	*Gives extra information – says when the Act was passed*
Quotation marks	reports to be published on the 'health' of UK zoos	*The inverted commas highlight the word because we are supposed to question its meaning here. The writer believes that the zoos are unhealthy – and suggests this by the use of inverted commas*
Equals sign	**SZ**= Small Zoo **W**= Wildlife/Safari Park	*The equals signs are a note form used in the key of the diagram to save the writer longer explanations*

Answers: Test Paper 8

Test Paper 8 Mark scheme: Questions and assessment focuses

Question	Describe, select and retrieve information and events or ideas from the text. Use quotation and reference to the text.	Deduce, infer and interpret information and events or ideas from the text.	Comment on the structure and organisation of texts, grammatical and presentational features at text level.	Comment on the writer's use of language, grammatical and literary features at word and sentence level.	Identify and comment on the writer's purposes and viewpoints, and the effect of the text on the reader.
			Focus and number of marks (G: includes a focus on grammar)		
1:1	1				
1:2	2				
1:3		1			
1:4				2 G	
1:5		2			
1:6	3				
1:7				2 G	
1:8					4
2:9	1				
2:10			1		
2:11			4		
2:12				3	
2:13				2	
2:14		2			
2:15		2			
2:16					4
3:17				1 G	
3:18	3				
3:19		2			
3:20					3
3:21			2 G		
3:22				3 G	
Total	**10**	**9**	**7**	**13**	**11**

Testing KS3 English Year 7 © Nelson Thornes 2003

Answers to Test Paper 9: Train journeys

Questions 1–8 are about *Just William on Holiday*

1   Copy and quote three clauses which express William's irresistible fascination with the train's communication cord.   **(1 mark)**
    Focus: Describe, select and retrieve information and events or ideas from the text. Use quotation and reference to the text.
    Any three from: 'Suddenly his eye lit on the notice', 'the fascination of it was more than he could resist', 'he fingered the chain, and imagined himself pulling it', 'There wouldn't be any harm in just pulling it a tiny bit'.

2   Give two examples from the passage which show that William has a strong imagination.   **(1 mark)**
    Focus: Describe, select and retrieve information and events or ideas from the text. Use quotation and reference to the text.
    Any two of the following: He pretended that it was the train which was stationary and that the countryside was moving past it; he pretended that he was a spy, a general on his way to war and a circus performer travelling to a show; he pretended he was a wizard who could make trees, fields and telegraph posts skip to his bidding.

3   Explain in your own words what made William pull the train's communication cord.   **(1 mark)**
    Focus: Deduce, infer and interpret information and events or ideas from the text.
    He was drawn to it as if by a magnet and could barely keep his hands off it as he wondered how it worked. He persuaded himself that if he pulled it only slightly the train would slow down just a little so that no one would notice.

4   How does the writer express how William felt after he pulled the communication cord?   **(2 marks)**
    Focus: Comment on the writer's use of language, grammatical and literary features at word and sentence level.
    William was horrified. The writer conjures up a picture of William, dumbstruck and shrinking into the corner of the carriage as if trying to make himself invisible: 'crouched in his corner of the carriage, frozen with horror'.

5   Explain William's bewilderment at what happened after he pulled the communication cord.   **(2 marks)**
    Focus: Deduce, infer and interpret information and events or ideas from the text.
    He did not realise that someone in the next carriage was being robbed, by coincidence, just before William pulled the cord. He wondered why the 'military-looking gentleman' had congratulated the guard on arriving so quickly.

6   List in chronological order the key events which took place on the train.   **(3 marks)**
    Focus: Describe, select and retrieve information and events or ideas from the text. Use quotation and reference to the text.
    William pulled the communication cord; the train stopped; the guard came running along the outside of the train; the military-looking gentleman began his story of having been robbed; the guard made enquiries as to who pulled the cord; everyone congratulated William.

7   Summarise the first three paragraphs of the passage and explain their purpose.   **(3 marks)**
    Focus: Comment on the structure and organisation of texts, grammatical and presentational features at text level.
    The first paragraph sets the scene (a train carriage) and gives the reader an idea about William's character (he is imaginative). The second paragraph explains why William is travelling alone, where he is going to and who will look after him. The third paragraph tells the reader about William's enjoyment of journeys. Together the three paragraphs provide a background to the story: what has happened already, whom it is about and where it takes place.

8   How does the writer communicate William's changing emotions throughout the journey?   **(4 marks)**
    Focus: Identify and comment on the writer's purposes and viewpoints, and the effect of the text on the reader.
    William begins by feeling quite interested in what is going on around him ('mildly interested' and 'amused himself'). He becomes more interested in his own imaginings and is almost carried away by make-believe (pretending to be a spy, a general and so on) and then becomes bored ('growing slightly bored'). Once he spots the communication cord he is fascinated ('the fascination of it was more than he could resist'), but after he pulls the cord he is scared ('frozen with horror'). As the story of the robbery in the next carriage emerges, William is relieved ('heaved a sigh of relief'), but then he is once again scared as the military-looking gentleman says he did not pull the cord and the guard's eyes are turned towards William ('frozen by horror once more', 'trying to efface himself'). He is bewildered when the guard congratulates him ('complete bewilderment') and then becomes smug ('assumed an air of modest heroism').
    The writer uses concise language to conjure up a picture of William, as described above, by saying what he does and how. The description of him after he leaves the train is a good example: 'He depreciated his exploit with airy gestures.'

Questions 9–16 are about *Adlestrop*

9   List three sounds which the poet heard at Adlestrop.   **(1 mark)**
    Focus: Describe, select and retrieve information and events or ideas from the text. Use quotation and reference to the text.
    Any three from: steam hissing, someone clearing his throat, a blackbird singing, and many other birds singing in the background.

10 What evidence can you find to show that, although it is short, this is a narrative as well as a descriptive poem?
    (2 marks)
    Focus: Comment on the structure and organisation of texts, grammatical and presentational features at text level.
    It is written in the past tense (for example, 'the express-train drew up there') and it recounts the events of the short episode in chronological order.

11 Describe Adlestrop and support your answer with quotations from the text.   **(1 mark)**
    Focus: Describe, select and retrieve information and events or ideas from the text. Use quotation and reference to the text.
    It is a small village (it must have few inhabitants because no one is seen in or around the station); it is in the country (the poet refers to the meadowsweet and haycocks he sees). It is in or near Oxfordshire or Gloucestershire (the poet hears, in the background of the blackbird's singing, 'all the birds of Oxfordshire and Gloucestershire').

12 Explain the effect on the reader of the writer's use of sentences which end in the middle of a line.   **(3 marks)**
    Focus: Comment on the structure and organisation of texts, grammatical and presentational features at text level.
    They give the poem a slow, measured pace and a feeling of stillness and quiet because they have the effect of making the reader read the lines slowly and hesitantly to see where the sentences are going to end, and then slowing down halfway through a line and starting again after the full stop.

13 'No whit less still and lonely fair ...'. What image does this line conjure up in your mind?   **(2 marks)**
    Focus: Comment on the writer's use of language, grammatical and literary features at word and sentence level.
    The line suggests that the station is deserted, and it is as if everything is hanging still in the air (like 'high cloudlets'). This gives the poem a quietness and stillness, but also an air of suspense; the poet seems to be wondering what will happen.

14 List the words in the poem which suggest the emptiness of the station at Adlestrop.   **(2 marks)**
    Focus: Comment on the writer's use of language, grammatical and literary features at word and sentence level.
    'No one left and no one came', 'the bare platform', 'only the name', 'lonely'.

15 What do you notice about the rhythm and pace of the poem and how this is created through the
    syllable-patterns of the words, the length of lines and the rhyme pattern?   **(3 marks)**
    Focus: Comment on structure and organisation of texts, grammatical and presentational features at text level.
    The rhythm is slow and measured. This is achieved partly by the use of sentences which continue from one line to the next. This slow and measured pace is accentuated by the rhyme pattern (the ends of the second and fourth line of each verse rhyme).

16 Describe the atmosphere of the station at Adlestrop and explain how the poet creates this atmosphere.
   Focus: Identify and comment on the writer's purposes and viewpoints, and the effect of the text on the reader. **(5 marks)**
   The station has a still, quiet and deserted atmosphere, which is created by the use of fairly long lines, which have a slow walking pace when read aloud, and the use of sentences which continue from one line (and even one verse) to the next. The sounds mentioned are muffled (even the hissing of steam seems quiet) and seem to linger on the air and then fade away. The use of polysyllabic words helps to create this stillness: words such as 'meadowsweet', 'unwontedly' and even the name of the station – 'Adlestrop'.

Questions 17–22 are about *the website of National Rail*

17 In what three ways do rail staff offer assistance to mobility-impaired or disabled passengers at their departure station? **(1 mark)**
   Focus: Describe, select and retrieve information and events or ideas from the text. Use quotation and reference to the text.
   They meet the passenger at the departure station, accompany the passenger to the train and see him or her safely on board.

18 Select three icons on the 'Useful Information' page on which you would click to help you to plan a journey on a weekday from your home to London (or, if you live in London, to Edinburgh), and say what kind of information you hope to find on each page. **(2 marks)**
   Focus: Describe, select and retrieve information and events or ideas from the text. Use quotation and reference to the text.
   Any three of the following: Conditions, Connections, Crossing London, Disabled Travel, Luggage/Pets, Maps, Reservations, Sleepers, Ticket Types, Traintaxi.

19 List three factors which affect the price of rail tickets. **(2 marks)**
   Focus: Deduce, infer and interpret information and events or ideas from the text.
   Any three of the following: the period within which the passenger will travel, the days of the week, the specific trains, booking in advance and travelling in a group.

20 Identify an example in the passage of the use of each of the following punctuation marks and explain why they are used: brackets, bullets and dashes. **(2 marks)**
   Focus: Comment on the writer's use of language, grammatical and literary features at word and sentence level.
   In the section 'Choosing Your Rail Ticket', under 'Special Tickets', the telephone number for National Rail Enquiries is placed within brackets so that the surrounding sentence can be read without interruption; the sentence makes sense without this additional piece of information, but it is placed where it is relevant. Bullets are used in the section entitled 'Passengers Needing Special Assistance' to highlight each action which travellers with disabilities or impaired mobility can take to facilitate their journey. In the introductory paragraph to the section 'Choosing Your Rail Ticket' the phrase 'together with links to their websites, where appropriate' is separated from the rest of the sentence by dashes. The use of dashes, like brackets, avoids disrupting the sense of the sentences and is a way of inserting extra information in the place where it is most relevant.

21 How well does the heading 'Choosing Your Rail Ticket' describe the page from which the information in the passage was taken, and how would you improve it? **(3 marks)**
   Focus: Comment on the structure and organisation of texts, grammatical and presentational features at text level.
   The information is helpful in telling you about the different kinds of tickets which are available. This means that you do not miss out on any special offers or buy a more expensive ticket than you need. However, you still need to find out what is available for your journey on the days when you want to travel.

22 How does the use of icons and other organisational features on this website help users to find the information they want? **(4 marks)**
   Focus: Identify and comment on the writer's purposes and viewpoints, and the effect of the text on the reader.
   Icons provide a quick visual guide to readers to help them to find the pages they need and to which they can move directly from any other page, without necessarily going back to the home page. Most icons, however, need some written explanation or heading; they do not completely replace text unless they are used very frequently (for example, an arrow to lead on to the next page). Underlining pieces of text and presenting them in blue tells the reader who is familiar with the Internet that they are to be clicked on to jump to other pages: for example, 'here' in the section on 'Passengers Needing Special Assistance', 'Train Companies' in 'Choosing Your Rail Ticket' and 'return to top' on any page. These work in the same way as icons.

Answers: Test Paper 9

Test Paper 9 Mark scheme: Questions and assessment focuses

Question	Describe, select and retrieve information and events or ideas from the text. Use quotation and reference to the text.	Deduce, infer and interpret information and events or ideas from the text.	Comment on the structure and organisation of texts, grammatical and presentational features at text level.	Comment on the writer's use of language, grammatical and literary features at word and sentence level.	Identify and comment on the writer's purposes and viewpoints, and the effect of the text on the reader.
			Focus and number of marks (G: includes a focus on grammar)		
1:1	1				
1:2	1				
1:3		1			
1:4				2	
1:5		2			
1:6	3				
1:7			3		
1:8					4
2:9	1				
2:10			2		
2:11	1				
2:12			3		
2:13				2	
2:14				2	
2:15			3		
2:16					5
3:17	1				
3:18	2				
3:19		2			
3:20				2 G	
3:21			3		
3:22					4
Total	10	5	14	8	13